A BOOK FOR
ALL SEASONS

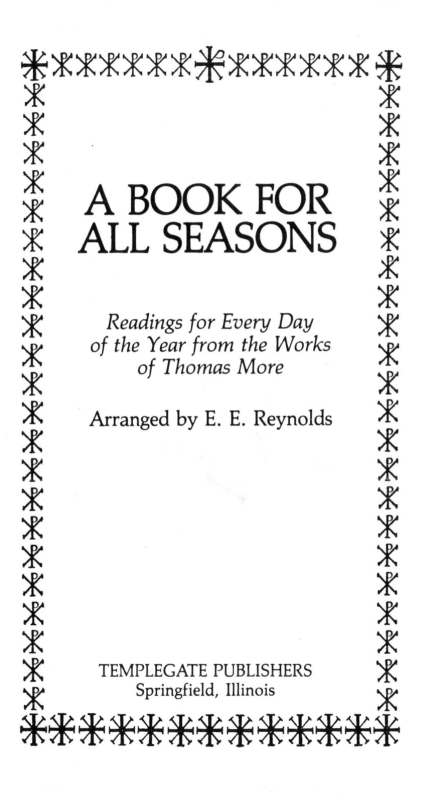

A BOOK FOR ALL SEASONS

*Readings for Every Day
of the Year from the Works
of Thomas More*

Arranged by E. E. Reynolds

TEMPLEGATE PUBLISHERS
Springfield, Illinois

Published 1978

Templegate Publishers

P.O. Box 5152

Springfield, Illinois

62705

This arrangement © E. E. Reynolds 1966

ISBN: 0-87243-184-3

Wood engraving by
Richard Shirley Smith

INTRODUCTION

Most of the extracts in this book are taken from *The Workes of Sir Thomas More Knyght, sometyme Lorde Chancellour of England, wrytten by him in the Englysh tonge*, a folio volume printed in London in 1557, and usually referred to as the *English Works*. It was edited by his nephew William Rastell. The remaining passages, a much smaller number, are from William Roper's *The Life of Syr Thomas More*. This book therefore consists of extracts chosen from St Thomas More's English writings, or from his reported words. Translations from the Latin writings, such as *Utopia* and many of his letters, are not included as it was felt that these would break the unity of the style.

At least half of the 1557 folio has not been reprinted since that date; in fact only *A Dialogue of Comfort* is easily accessible. Other works have been issued in limited or scholarly editions; in time all will be available in the Yale Edition. Over a hundred passages in the present volume are here reprinted for the first time in four centuries, and it is hoped that one value of the selection will prove to be the introduction of the reader to hitherto scarcely known treasures from the writings of St Thomas More.

His prose does not make easy reading. He was writing at a period when English as a written and printed language was still in its formative stage. The order of words is sometimes strange to us, and his sentences are often complicated by long digressions that break the thought, so that close attention is needed if the thread is not to be lost. There is little that punctuation can do to ease the reader's task. The close attention needed will be amply rewarded. The more archaic words have been replaced by modern equivalents. The scholar will frown at this, but this book is intended not only for him but for ordinary folk. He can turn to the original by following up the reference number given at the end of each extract. This refers to the page of the *English Works*, or, if with an asterisk, to William Roper's *Life* in the Everyman's Library edition. The title of the work from which an extract had been taken can be learned from the following list of the contents of the *English Works*.

Page　　　　　　　　　　*Title*

1. Life of John Picus.
35. King Richard III.
72. Four Last Things.
105. Dialogue concerning Heresies. *
288. Supplication of Souls. *
339. Confutation of Tyndale's Answer. *
833. Letter impugning... John Frith. *
845. Apology. *
929. Debellation of Salem and Bizance. *
1033. First Part of Poisoned Book. *
1139. Dialogue of Comfort.
1264. The Blessed Body of Our Lord.
1270. Passion of Christ.
1405. Prayers and meditations.
1422. Letters.

* = controversial

About two thirds of the *English Works* is made up of controversial writings. Much of this has lost its point as the grounds of argument shift from century to century; we no longer, for instance, get heated in discussing the accuracy of Tyndale's translation of the New Testament. Sometimes a topic may still have an interest, as, for instance, the following comment by More on the use of English in the liturgy.

> And surely if all the service were in English yet would it not thereby be much the more understood, which was all the matter that St Paul spake (1. Cor. 14). For many that now do understand the Latin tongue do little yet understand the sentence [meaning] farther than the bare stories and collects. *(English Works,* p. 414).

The extract given under 12th November suggests that More would have accepted recent Council decisions and would not have been found among the "few wilful folk" who still protest. His views on "common war" (17th November) bear on another present-day question.

As the reader of the controversial works plods his way through the polemic sands, he will come across oases that make the journey worth while. Sometimes it is a passage giving More's thought on an aspect of the faith; sometimes it is an expression of his wisdom in the ways of his fellow men, or a reminiscence of his own experiences; our attention may be caught by a happy similitude, or by one of those humourous turns of phrase so characteristic of him, for his sense of humour was never far below the surface. He found it difficult to resist telling a "merry tale" even if not strictly apposite, or, to use an outmoded term, edifying. Examples of all these will be found in the following pages, but the main emphasis in making the selection has been on More's teaching on religion and the life of the spirit. Some themes recur time and again. Devotion to the Blessed Sacrament runs like a silver thread through

More's meditations; a frequent thought is the transient nature of human life and the folly of clinging to our earthly possessions. He wrote much on the reading and study of the Scriptures as this was a main controversial subject of the time; here he reiterated that the authority of the Church must control the personal judgment of the reader. The Church and the Early Fathers were among his favourite subjects, and we may note how great a part St Augustine played in his thought. Above all he wrote of our dependence on the grace that God bestows upon us; this was the leading thought of his meditations in the Tower.

"Give me the grace, good Lord, to set the world at nought."

"The things, good Lord, that I pray for, give me thy grace to labour for."

Since many of these extracts are drawn from unfamiliar sources, it is hoped that they will give readers a wider view of St Thomas More's personality and spirituality. It proved difficult to group the passages satisfactorily under subject headings, so the material has been arranged as a series of daily readings. The subject index will enable the reader to follow More's thought on any particular theme.

E.E.R.

JANUARY

1. *O glorious blessed Trinity, whose justice hath damned unto perpetual pain many proud rebellious angels, whom thy goodness had created to be partners of thine eternal glory, for thy tender mercy plant in mine heart such meekness that I so may by thy grace follow the prompting of my good angel, and so resist the proud suggestions of those spiteful spirits that fell, as I may, through the merits of thy bitter passion, be partner of thy bliss with those holy spirits that stood and now, confirmed by thy grace, in glory shall stand for ever.*[1] *(1273)*

2. Yea verily, good readers, to believe well is no little work, and so great a work that no man can do it of his own strength without the special help of God. *(1048)*

3. God knew that it was nothing meet for servant to stand in better condition than his master, as our Lord saith himself in the Gospel. And therefore would he not suffer that while he came to his own kingdom not without travail and pain, his servant should be slothful and sit and pick his nails and be carried up to heaven at their ease, but biddeth every man that will be his disciple or servant, take up his cross upon his back, and therewith come forth and follow him. *(1290)*

4. He that by good use and experience hath in his eye the right mark and very true lustre of the diamond, rejecteth anon and listeth not to look upon the counterfeit, be it never so well handled, never so craftily polished.

---

[1] The italicized passages are prayers and meditations composed in the Tower, 1534-5.

And trust it well that, in likewise, if men would well accustom themselves in the taste of spiritual pleasure and of that sweet feeling that virtuous people have of the good hope of heaven, they should shortly set at nought, and at length abhor, the foul delight and filthy liking that riseth of sensual and fleshly pleasure, which is never so pleasantly spiced with delight and liking but that it bringeth therewith such a murmuring and grief of conscience that it maketh the stomach heave and bid fair to vomit. *(73)*

5. Mark how the church is made without spot or wrinkle. She is stretched out in the stretcher of the cross, as a church well washed and cleansed. *(797)*

6. The Church of Christ hath been, is, and ever shall be, taught and instructed by God and his Holy Spirit with his holy word of either kind, that is to say both with his written word and his word unwritten, and that they which will not believe God's word but if he put it in writing, be as plain infidels as they that will not believe it written, since God's word taketh his authority of God that speaketh it and not of man that writeth it. *(445)*

7. *The souls in Purgatory speak :*
And forasmuch as ye never can conceive a very right imagination of these things which ye never felt, nor it is not possible to find you any example in the world very like unto the pains that pious souls feel when they be departed thence, we shall therefore put you in remembrance of one kind of pain which though it be nothing like for the quantity of the matter, yet may it somewhat be resembled by reason of the fashion and manner. If there were embarked many people at once to be by ship conveyed a long way by sea of such as never came

thereon before, and should happen all the way to have the seas rise high and sore wrought, and sometime soon upon a storm to be long after wallowing at an anchor, there should ye find divers fashions of folks. Some peradventure (but of them very few) so clean from all evil humours and so well attempered of themself, that they shall be all that long voyage by sea as lusty and jocund as of they were on land. But far the most part shall ye see foresicke, and yet in many sundry manner, some more, some less, some longer time diseased and some much sooner amended, and divers that awhile had thought they should have died for pain, yet after once vomit or twain so clear rid of their grief that they never feel displeasure of it after. And this happeth after as the body is more or less disposed in itself thereto. But then shall ye sometime see there some other whose body is so incurably corrupted that they shall reel and stagger and wring their hands and gnash the teeth and their eyes water, their head ache, their body fret, their stomach heave, and all their body shiver for pain and yet shall never vomit at all, or if they vomit, yet shall they vomit still and never find ease thereof. Lo thus fareth it as a small thing may be resembled to a great by ye souls deceased and departed the world; that such as be clean and unspotted can in the fire feel no disease at all and on the other side such as come thence so deadly poisoned within, that their spots be indelible and their filthiness unpurgeable, lie fretting and frying in the fire for ever. And only such as neither be fully cleaned nor yet sore defiled but that the fire may burn out the spots of their sin; of this sort only be we that here lie in Purgatory. *(321)*

8. And yet since there is no man for all that so old, but that he hopeth yet that he may live one year more,

and of a frail folly delighteth to think thereon, and comforting himself therewith; other men's words of like manner comfort, adding more sticks to that fire, shall in manner burn up quite the pleasant moisture that most should refresh him, the wholesome dew (I mean) of God's grace, by which he should wish with God's will to be hence, and long to be with him in heaven. *(1139)*

9. For any one plain text of scripture sufficeth for the proof of any truth, except any man be of the mind that he will have God tell his tale twice ere he believe him. *(324)*

10. Ye shall good Christian readers understand that like as if a man would teach a child to read, he must first begin his A.B.C. (for without the knowledge of his letters he can never go forward); so forasmuch as no man can come unto Christ without faith, but faith must needs be the first step toward all Christian virtues since no man can hope in him or love him whom he knoweth not, and Christ can no man Christianly know, but by faith (for as St Paul saith, he that cometh unto God, he must needs believe) so did Our Saviour therefore as a good and wise master of his Christian school, begin there with the Jews that there offered themselves as his scholars, he began, I say, with faith. *(1049)*

11. How can you be comfortless in any tribulation, when Christ and his Holy Spirit, and with them their unseparable Father (if you put full trust and confidence in them) be never neither one finger breadth of space nor one minute of time from you? *(1140)*

12. For what thing is there that better tameth the flesh than the grace of God? Did not God answer

St Paul when he thrice prayed him to withdraw the thorn in the flesh (2 Cor. 12, 7) with which our Lord suffered the angel of Satan to vex him, lest his heart might grow too high and wax proud in beholding the marvellous greatness of his revelations, which though some good men take for some other kind of tribulation, I see not why it might not be the very fleshly motion against his vow of chastity, did not our Lord, I say, make him answer in this wide, "Sufficeth unto thee my grace"? *(413)*

13. Let us therefore leave the devil's deceitful service and take nothing at his hand. For he nothing giveth but trifles; nor giveth half an inch of pleasure without one whole ell of pain. *(1305)*

14. For likewise as pride threw down the devil out of heaven, so shall there never no one ascend but with meekness thither. *(1320)*

15. For though it be very true that without God's help and God's grace predisposing or preceding, no man can believe, yet if there were nothing in the man himself whereby he might receive it, if he would, with grace, which God of his goodness offereth, apply himself towardly to the receiving thereof, and whereby on the other side he might perversely refuse it, or of sloth and negligence so slightly regard it that he were worthy to lose it, if there were, I say, no such thing in the man whereby he himself might somewhat do therein with God, Our Lord would not call upon men and exhort them to believe and praise them that will believe, and rebuke them that will not believe, as he doth in many plain places of the Scripture. *(580)*

16. They receive the blessed body of Our Lord both sacramentally and virtually which in due manner and worthily receive the blessed sacrament. When I say worthily I mean not that any man is so good, or can be so good, that his goodness could make him of very right reason and worthy to receive into his vile earthly body that holy blessed glorious flesh and blood of Almighty God himself, with his celestial soul therein and with the majesty of his eternal godhead, but that he may prepare himself, working with the grace of God, to stand in such a state as the incomparable goodness of God will, of his liberal bounty, vouchsafe to take and accept for worthy to receive his own inestimable precious body into the body of so simple a servant. *(1264)*

17. *O Holy Trinity, the Father, the Son, and the Holy Ghost, three equal and coeternal Persons, and one Almighty God, have mercy on me, vile, abject, abominable, sinful wretch: meekly acknowledging before thine High Majesty my long-continued sinful life, even from my very childhood hitherto. (1417)*

18. Albeit great sin it is for any vicious person to take upon him the office of a preacher and to presume to tell other folk their faults before he mend his own, for as much as if his audience may take occasion of his evil living to have the truth in contempt, yet may they rather list to take good than harm, find therein a great occasion the more strongly to confirm them in the truth. *(704)*

19. A faint faith is better than a strong heresy. *(423)*

20. And therefore is Holy Scripture the highest and the best learning that any man can have, if one take the

right way in the learning. It is, as a good holy saint saith, so marvellously tempered that a mouse may wade therein, and an elephant be drowned therein. For there is no man so low but if he will seek his way with the staff of his faith in his hand, and hold that fast and search the way therewith, and have the old holy fathers also for his guides, going on with a good purpose and a lowly heart, using reason and refusing no good learning with calling of God for wisdom, grace and help, that he may well keep his way and follow his good guides, then shall he never fall in peril, but well and surely wade through and come to such end of his journey as himself would well wish. *(162)*

21. And when men come together to honour God, each of them is profitable to other, for else were their assembly together in prayer no difference from the prayer of one man alone. But when they come together to God's service, the whole company prayeth for the whole presence, and so is everyeach the better for others prayer and all the people the better both for the prayer and the sacrament, and every devout observance used in the Church at divine service. *(413)*

22. Let us require the high physician, our blessed Saviour Christ, whose holy manhood God ordained for our necessity, to cure our deadly wounds with the medicine made of the most wholesome blood of his own blessed body; that likewise as he cured by that incomparable medicine our mortal malady, it may like him to send us and put in our minds such medicines at this time, as against the sickness and sorrows of tribulations may so comfort and strength us in his grace, as our deadly enemy the devil may never have the power by his poisoned dart of murmur, grudge, and impatience,

to turn our short sickness of worldly tribulation into the endless everlasting death of infernal damnation. *(1142)*

23. Whereas the sacrament of baptism is not called the sacrament alone, but the sacrament of baptism, nor any of the remnant without the addition of their own proper name, as the sacrament of confirmation, the sacrament of penance, and so forth the remnant, only the blessed sacrament is called and known by the name of sacrament alone, signifying and showing thereby that this blessed sacrament is the most excellent and of all holy sacraments the chief. *(1337)*

24. If we would not suffer the strength and fervour of our faith to wax lukewarm, or rather key-cold, and in manner lose his vigour by scattering our minds abroad about so many trifling things, that of the matters of our faith we very seldom think, but that we would withdraw our thought from the respect and regard of all worldly fantasies, and so gather our faith together into a little narrow room, and like the little grain of mustard seed, which is of nature hot, set it in the garden of our soul, all weeds pulled out for the better feeding of our faith; then shall it grow, and so spread up in height, that the birds, that is to say, the holy angels of heaven, shall breed in our soul and bring forth virtues in the branches of our faith. And then with the faithful trust that through the true belief of God's word we shall put in his promise, we shall be well able to command a great mountain of tribulation to quit the place where he stood in our heart; whereas, with a very feeble faith and a faint, we shall be scarcely able to remove a little hillock. *(1143)*

25. Bear no malice nor evil will to no man living. For

either the man is good or nought. If he be good, and I hate him, then am I nought. If he be nought, either he shall amend and die good and go to God, or abide nought and die nought and go to the Devil. And then let me remember that if he shall be saved, he shall not fail (if I be saved too, as I trust to be) to love me very heartily and I shall then in likewise love him. And why should I now then hate one for this while which shall hereafter love me for evermore, and why should I be now enemy to him with whom I shall in time coming be coupled in eternal friendship? And on the other side, if he shall continue nought and be damned, that is there so outrageous eternal sorrow towards him, that I may well think myself a deadly cruel wretch if I would not now rather pity his pain than malign his person. *(1421)*

26. When men endeavour themself toward so good a thing, they may then make themselve sure that God hath predisposed them with his grace, for else they could not so do, and that he is ready with his grace to walk forward with them. *(581)*

27. The Messenger maketh objection that miracles shewed before a multitude may be feigned. — This is, quod I, very truth that such things may be and sometime so be indeed. As I remember me that I have heard my father tell of a beggar that in King Henry, his days, the sixth, came with his wife to Saint Alban's, and there was walking about the town begging a five or six days before the King's coming thither, saying that he was born blind and never saw in his life. And was warned in his dream that he should come out of Berwick, where he said he had ever dwelled, to seek

Saint Alban, and that he had been at his shrine and had not been helped. And therefore he would go seek him at some other place. For he had heard some say since he came that Saint Alban's body should be at Cologne, and indeed such a contention hath there been. But of truth, as I am surely informed, he lieth here at Saint Alban's, saving some relics of him which they there shew shrined. But to tell you forth when the King was come, and the town full, suddenly this man at Saint Alban's shrine, had his sight again, and a miracle solemnly rung and *Te Deum* sung, so that nothing was talked of in all the town but this miracle. So happened it, that Duke Humfrey of Gloucester, a great wise man and very learned, having great joy to see such a miracle, called that poor man unto him. And first showing himself joyous of God's glory, so showed in the getting of his sight, and exhorting him to meekness, and to none ascribing of any part of the worship to himself nor to be proud of the people's praise which would call him a good and a godly man thereby. At last he looked well upon his eyes, and asked him whether he could never see nothing at all in all his life before. And when as well his wife as himself affirmed readily no, then he looked intently upon his eyes again, and said, "I believe you very well, for me thinketh that ye cannot see well yet."

"Yes, Sir," quod he, "I thank God and his holy martyr, I can now see as well as any man".

"Ye can", quod the Duke. "What colour is my gown?" Then anon the beggar told him.

"What colour", quod he, "is this man's gown?" He told him also, and so forth without any hesitation, he told him the names of all the colours that could be shewed him. And when my lord saw that, he bade him walk impostor and made him be set openly in the stocks. For though he could have seen suddenly by miracle the difference between divers colours, yet could he not by sight so suddenly tell the names of all these colours but if he had known them before, no more than the names of all the men that he should suddenly see. *(134)*

28. How much need have we poor wretches that shall die ere we would, and cannot tell the time when, but peradventure this present day, what need have we I say to make haste about these things that we must needs do, so that we may nothing left undone when we be suddenly sent for and must needs go. *(1218)*

29. Yet is not reason alway to be mistrusted where faith standeth not against it, nor God saith not the contrary. Except reason be so far out of credence with you that ye will not now believe him if he tell you that twice twain make four, I suppose you will manage by reason as one did once by a false knave. He sware that he would not for twenty pounds hear him say his creed. For he knew him for such a liar that he thought he should never believe his creed after, if he heard it once of his mouth. Howbeit, quod I, let us yet see whether God himself in Scripture tell you the same tale or no. God telleth you in Scripture that he would be with his Church to the end of the world. I think ye doubt not thereof but those words he spoke to the whole Church that then was and ever shall be from the apostles' days continued till the end of the world.

That in good faith, quod he, must needs be so.

Then were this in good faith enough, quod I, for our purpose, since no man doubteth wherefore he will be with his Church; except we should think that he would be therewith for nothing, wherefore should he be with it but to keep it and preserve it with the assistance of his gracious presence from spiritual mischief specially, and of all other, especially from infidelity and from idolatry—which was the special thing from which he called his Church out of the Gentiles which else as for moral virtues and political, if they had not lacked the right cause and end of referring their acts to God, were many of them not far under many of us. Let us go further. Doth he not in the fourteenth, fifteenth and sixteenth chapters of Saint John again and again repeat that after his going he will come again to them? And saith he will not leave them orphans as fatherless children; but will come again to them himself. Let us add now thereunto the words before rehearsed, that he will be with them till the world's end, and it appeareth plain that he meant all this by his whole Church that should be to the world's end. When he said unto them, "I call you friends, for all that I have heard of my Father I have made knowen unto you," (John 15, 15) he spake as to his perpetual Church and not to the apostles alone, but if he said it to them alone these words also, "I command that ye love each other," (John 13,34) so that none should love each other after but only they. Now lest the things that he taught them should by the Church after be forgotten, which was more to be doubted than of themself that heard it, he said unto them also, "These things", quod he, "have I spoken to you abiding here with you. But the Comforter which is the Holy Ghost (whom my Father shall send in my name) he shall teach you all thing, and he shall put you in mind and remembrance of all thing that I shall have said unto you" (John 14, 26). So that here ye see that he shall again alway teach the Church of new, the old lessons of Christ. And he said also to them, that this comforter, this Holy Ghost, the spirit of truth, should be sent to abide with them for ever, which cannot be meant but of the whole Church. For the Holy Ghost was not sent hither into the earth here to dwell with the apostles for ever, for they dwelled not so long here. Now if the spirit of truth shall dwell in the Church for ever, how can the Church err in perceiving of the truth in such things I mean as God will bind them to know or shall be necessary for them to know? For only of such things meant Our Lord when he said that the Holy Ghost shall teach them all thing. For as Saint Paul saith, the manifestation and shewing of the spirit is to the utility and profit. (1 Cor. 12, 7). This Holy Spirit also was not promised by Our Saviour Christ that he should only tell his Church again his words; but he said further, "I have", quod he, "besides all this many things to say to you, but ye be not able to bear them now. But when he shall come that is the spirit of truth, he shall lead you unto all truth" (John 16, 13). Lo, Our Lord said not that the Holy Ghost should write unto his Church all truth, but that he should lead them by secret inspiration and inclination of their hearts into all truth—in which must needs be conceived both information and right belief of every necessary article, and of the right and true sense of Holy Scripture as far as shall be requisite to conserve the Church from any damnable error. *(173)*

30. This virtue of faith can neither any man give himself, nor yet any one man another; but though men may with preaching be ministers unto God therein, and the man with his own free-will obeying freely the inward inspiration of God be a weak worker with Almighty God therein, yet is faith indeed the gracious gift of God himself. For, as St James saith, "Every good gift and every perfect gift is given from above,

descending from the Father of lights" (James 1, 17). Therefore, feeling our faith by many tokens very faint, let us pray him that giveth it, that it may please him to help and increase it. And let us first say with him in the Gospel, "I believe, good Lord, but help thou the lack of my belief" (Mark 9, 24). And after let us pray with the Apostles, "Lord, increase our faith" (Luke 17, 5). *(1143)*

31. The Scripture is full of those places by which it plainly appeareth that God looketh of duty, not only that we should amend and be better in the time to come, but also be sorry, and weep, and bewail our sins committed before, and all the holy doctors be full and whole of that mind, that men must have for their sins contrition and sorrow of heart. *(1176)*

FEBRUARY

1. *Almighty God, that of thine infinite goodness didst create our first parents in the state of innocence, with present wealth and hope of heaven to come, till through the devil's guile their folly fell by sin to wretchedness, for thy tender pity of that passion that was paid for their and our redemption, assist me so with thy gracious help, that unto the subtle suggestions of the serpent I never so incline the ears of mine heart but that my reason may resist them and master my sensuality and refrain me from them. (1279)*

2. For the lack of spiritual eating, the fleshly eater of his flesh, though he receive the sacrament, receiveth not the effect of the sacrament, the thing that the sacrament signifieth, that is the participation of the mystical body of Christ, that is to say the Church and congregation of all saints, which Church and congregation is gathered together as many members into one body Christ as the head which our Lord in the sacrament changed into his blessed body, is one loaf made of many grains of wheat and the wine which he changeth into his blood, is one cup of wine made of many grapes. *(1067)*

3. For like as the ground that is all choked with nettles, briars, and other evil weeds, can bring forth no corn till they be weeded out, so can our soul have no place for the good corn of spiritual pleasure as long as it is overgrown with the barren weeds of carnal delectation. For the pulling out of which weeds by the root, there is not a more meet instrument than the remembrance of the four last things—death, doom, pain, and joy—which as they shall pull out these

weeds of fleshly voluptuousness, so shall they not fail to plant in their places, not only wholesome virtues, but also marvellous spiritual pleasure and spiritual gladness, which in every good soul riseth of the love of God, and hope of heaven, and inward liking that the godly spirit taketh in the diligent labour or good and virtuous business. *(74)*

4. As it were utterly vain to lay natural reasons of comfort to him that hath no wit, so were it undoubtedly frustrate to lay spiritual causes of comfort to him that hath no faith. For except a man first believe that Holy Scripture is the word of God, and that the word of God is true, how can a man take any comfort of that that the Scriptures telleth him therein? *(1143)*

5. And St Thomas Aquinas said that proper pleasant talking is a good virtue, serving to refresh the mind and make it quick and lusty to labour and study again, where continual weariness would make it dull and deadly. *(1171)*

6. The Church of Christ hath been, is, and ever shall be, taught and instructed by God and his Holy Spirit with his holy word of either kind, that is to say both with his word written and his word unwritten, and that they which will not believe God's word but if he put it into writing, be as plain infidels as they that will not believe it written, since God's word taketh his authority of God that speaketh it and not of man that writeth it. *(445)*

7. The covetous man, because he never ceaseth to dote upon his goods, and is ever alike greedy thereupon, whoso giveth him advice to be liberal seemeth to preach

to a glutton for fasting when his belly is empty and gapeth for good meat, or to a lewd fornicator when his trollop is lately light in his lap. Hardly can death cure them when he cometh. I remember me of a thief once condemned at Newgate, that cut a purse at the bar when he should be hanged on the morrow; and when he was asked why he did so, knowing that he should die shortly, the desperate wretch said that it did his heart good to be lord of that purse one night yet. And in good faith, methinketh as much as we wonder at him, yet see we many that do much like, of whom we nothing wonder at all. I let pass old priests that sue for advowsons of younger priests' benefices. I let pass old men that sigh and long to be executors to some that be younger than themselves: whose goods, if they would fall, they reckon would do them good to have in their keeping yet one year ere they die. But look if ye see not some wretch that scarcely can creep for age, his head hanging in his bosom, and his body crooked, walk pit-pat upon a pair of pattens with the staff in one hand and the *pater noster* in the other hand, the one foot almost in the grave already, and yet never the more haste to part with anything, nor to restore that he hath evil gotten, but as greedy to get a fourpenny piece by the beguiling of his neighbour as if he had of certainty seven score years to live. *((93)*

8. To believe meritoriously, so as it shall be rewarded with salvation, may not be faith alone, but faith with a working love. Nor it may not be a bare believing of Christ, but it must be a believing in Christ, that is, as St Augustine saith, not an idle dead standing belief, but a belief lively, quick and stirring and by charity and good works ever walking and going with Christ. *(1050)*

9. The name of Housel doth not only signify unto us the blessed body and blood of our Lord in the sacramental form, but also—like as this English word God signifieth unto us not only the unity of the Godhead, but also the Trinity of the three persons, and not only their super-substantial substance, but also every gracious property, as Justice, Mercy, Truth, Almightiness, Eternity, and every good thing more than we can imagine—so doth unto us English folk this English word Housel, though not express yet imply, and under a reverent, devout silence signify, both the sacramental signs and the sacramental things, as well as the things contained as the things holily signified, with all the secret unsearchable mysteries of the same. All which holy things right many persons, very little learned, but yet in grace godly minded, with heart humble and religious, not arrogant, proud and curious, under the name of holy Housel, with inward heavenly comfort, do full devoutly reverence. *(1339)*

10. A lewd gallant and a friar: whom when the gallant saw going barefoot in a great frost and snow, he asked him why he did take so much pain. And he answered that it was very little pain if a man would remember hell. "Yea, friar," quoth the gallant, "but what an there be none hell, then art thou a great fool." "Yea, master," quoth the friar, "but what an there be hell, then is your mastership a much more fool." *(329)*

11. "I thank our Lord, son, I find his Grace [the King] my very good lord indeed, and I believe he doth as singularly favour me as any subject in this realm. Howbeit, son Roper, I may tell thee, I have no cause to be proud thereof, for if my head could win him a castle in France, it should not fail to go." *(12*)*

12. Since nothing can better tame the flesh than the grace of God, which not only can tame it but also make the rebellion thereof so resisted by the soul that the fight shall turn the man to merit and reward, why shall not then such observances as the Spirit of God hath taught us to serve him with, and which obediently done with devotion and with desire of grace, do stand in the stead of one of the most effectual kinds of prayer, so profitable to the taming of the flesh, and either cause it the less to rebel, or else, which is yet happily better, strength the soul in such wise against the rebellion of the flesh, that by the valiant resisting thereof, it may have the more glorious triumph and victory. *(413)*

13. And God give us all the grace to do all our business in time that we spend not our time in vanities, or worse than vanities, while we be in health and drive off the things of substance we should do, till we lie in our deathbed where we shall have so many things to do at once and everything so unready that every finger shall be a thumb, and we shall fumble it up in haste unhandsomely that we may chance, but if God help the better, to leave more than half undone. *(1299)*

14. No man ought to doubt but that with prayers of the Church and with wholesome sacrifice, and with alms that is given for the souls of them that are departed, they are helped to be more mercifully dealt with of our Lord than their sins have deserved. For this thing by the tradition of the old fathers of the whole Catholic Church observeth that is to say, that what time they that deceased in the communion of blood of Christ at the time of the sacrifice in their place and order, remembrance made of them, prayer should be made for them and not that only but also that special rehearsal should

be made that the same sacrifice is offered for them too. Now when works of mercy are done in commendation and favour of them, who can doubt but that they are helped therewith, since prayer made for them unto God is not fruitless? *(800)*

15. But here consider this, that I speak here of him that in tribulation longeth to be comforted by God; and it is he that referreth the manner of his comforting to God, holding content, whether it be by the taking away or the diminishment of the tribulation itself or by the giving him patience and spiritual consolation therein. For of him that only longeth to have God take his trouble from him, we cannot so well warrant that mind for a cause of so great comfort. For both may he desire that, that never mindeth to be the better; and may miss also the effect of his desire, because his request is perhaps not good for himself. *(1144)*

16. How can we doubt that God delighteth to be with the sons of men, when the Son of God, and very Almighty God himself liked not only to become the son of man, that is to wit, the son of Adam the first man, but over that in his innocent manhood to suffer his painful passion for the redemption and restitution of man. In remembrance and memorial whereof, he disdaineth not to take for worthy such men as wilfully make not themselves unworthy to receive the self-same blessed body into their bodies, to the inestimable wealth of their souls. And yet of his high sovereign patience he refuseth not to enter bodily into the vile bodies of those whose filthy minds refuse to receive him graciously into their souls. But then do such folk receive him only sacramentally and not virtually. That is to wit, they receive his very blessed body into theirs

under the sacramental sign, but they receive not the thing of the sacrament, that is to say, the virtue and the effect thereof, that is to say, the grace by which they should be lively members incorporate in Christ's holy mystical body, but instead of that live grace they receive their judgement and their damnation. *(1264)*

17. *Now, good gracious Lord, as thou givest me thy grace to acknowledge my sins, so give me thy grace, not in only word but in heart also with very sorrowful contrition to repent them and utterly to forsake them. And forgive me those sins also, in which by mine own default, through evil disposition and evil custom, my reason is with sensuality so blinded that I cannot discern them for sin. And illumine, good Lord, mine heart, and give me thy grace to to know them, and forgive me my sins negligently forgotten, and bring them to my mind with grace to be purely confessed of them. (1417)*

18. The devil is ready to put out men's eyes that are content willingly to become blind. *(341)*

19. Whoso be fallen into a deep pit and thence drawn out, is not drawn from the brink but from the bottom. And so likewise God that draweth, draweth even from the beginning and casteth down the cord of his grace to take hold upon, whereupon whoso taketh hold and holdeth still, is by God drawn unto God and helpeth himself to be drawn. *(712)*

20. Fasting is better than eating, and more thank hath of God, and yet will God that we shall eat. Praying is better than drinking, and much more pleasant to God, and yet will God that we shall drink. Waking in good business is much more acceptable to God than

sleeping, and yet will God that we shall sleep. God hath given us our bodies here to keep, and will that we maintain them to do him service with till he send for us hence. *(1160)*

21. And therefore, as I say, whoso hath such a trouble of his scrupulous conscience, let him for a while forbear the judgment of himself and follow the counsel of some other whom he knoweth for well learned and virtuous and specially in the place of confession. For there is God specially present with his grace, assisting his holy sacrament. And let him not doubt to acquit his mind, and follow that he there is bidden, and think for a while less of the fear of God's justice, and be more merry in the remembrance of his mercy, and persevere in prayer for grace and abide and dwell faithfully in the sure hope of his help. And then shall he find, without any doubt, that the shield of God's truth shall, as the prophet saith, so compass him about that he shall not dread this night's fear of scrupulosity, but shall have afterward his conscience established in good quiet and rest. *(1186)*

22. For what free man is there so free that can be suffered to do what him pleases? In many things God hath restrained us by his high commandment, so many, that of those things which else we would do, I think it be more than half. Howbeit, because, God forgive us, we omit so little therefore but do what we please, as though we heard him not, we reckon our liberty never the less for that. But then is our liberty much restrained by the laws made by men for the quiet and politic governance of the people. And these would, I think, let our liberty but a little neither, were it not for fear of the pains that fall thereupon. Look, then, whether other

men, that have authority over us, command us never no business which we dare not but do, and therefore do it full oft full sore against our wills. Of which things some service is sometime so painful and so perilous too, that no lord can lightly command his bondman worse, nor seldom doth command him half so sore. Let every free man that reckoneth his liberty to stand in doing what he pleases, consider well these points, and I think he shall then find his liberty much less than he took it for before.

And yet have I left untouched the bondage that almost every man is in that boasteth himself for free, the bondage, I mean, of sin, which to be a very bondage, I shall have Our Saviour himself to bear me good record. For he saith "Every man that committeth sin, is the thrall, or the bondman of sin" (John 8, 34). And then if this be thus (and it must needs so be sith God saith it is so) who is there then that may make so much boast of his liberty, that he should take it for so sore a thing and so strange, to become through chance of war bond unto a man, while he is already through sin become willingly thrall and bond unto the devil? *(1238)*

23. For likewise as though a sophist would with a foolish argument prove unto a simple soul that two eggs were three because that there is one, and there be two, and one and twain make three, that simple unlearned man, though he lack learning to refute his fond argument, hath yet wit enough to laugh thereat and eat the two eggs himself and bid the sophist take and eat the third, so is every faithful man as sure in the sight of his soul, how apparently soever an heretic argue by Scripture to the contrary, that the common faith of Christ's Catholic Church is out of question true, and that the Scripture understanden right, is never thereto contrary, since he knows well both by his

faith and by the Scripture that the Church is taught his faith by God and his Holy Spirit according to Christ's promise that can never be false. *(475)*

24. Whether a man should cast in his mind and appoint in his heart before, that if he were taken with Turks, he would rather die than forsake his faith:—to counsel a man never to think on that case, is in my mind as much reason as the medicine that I have heard taught one for the tooth-ache, to go thrice about a churchyard and never think on a fox-tail. For if the counsel be not given them, it cannot serve them; and if it be given them, it must put the point of the matter in their mind, which by and by to reject, and think therein neither one thing nor other, is a thing that may be sooner bidden than obeyed. I think also that very few men can escape it, but that though they would never think thereon by themself, yet in one place or other, where they shall happen to come in company, they shall have the question by chance so proposed and put forth, that like as while he heareth one talking to him, he may well wink if he will but he cannot make himself sleep; so shall he, whether he will or no, think one thing or other therein. Finally, when Christ spake so often and so plain of the matter, that every man should upon pain of damnation openly confess his faith, if men took him and by dread of death would drive him to the contrary, it seemeth me in a manner implied therein that we be bounden conditionally to have evermore that mind, actually sometime and evermore habitually, that if the case so should fall, then, with God's help, so we would. And thus much thinketh me necessary for every man and woman to be always of this mind and often to think thereupon. *(1215)*

25. They that receive our Lord by the sacrament only, and not by faith and purpose of amendment, though they receive him, yet they receive him not, and though they eat him, they eat him not. *(1066)*

26. But now must you consider that though prosperity be contrary to tribulation, yet unto many a good man the devil's temptation unto pride in prosperity, is a greater tribulation and more need hath of good comfort and good counsel both, than he that never felt it would think. And that is the thing that maketh me speak thereof as of a thing proper to this matter. For as it is a thing right hard to touch pitch and never defile the fingers, to put flax into fire and yet keep them from burning, to keep a serpent in thy bosom and yet be safe from stinging, to put young men with young women without danger of foul fleshly desire, so is it hard for any person either man or woman, in great wordly wealth and much prosperity, so to withstand the suggestions of the devil and occasions given by the world that they keep themself from the deadly desire of ambitious glory. Whereupon there followeth, if a man fall thereto, an whole flood of all unhappy mischief, arrogant manner, high, sullen, solemn bearing, overlooking the poor in word and countenance, displeasant and disdainful behaviour, rapine, extortion, oppression, hatred and cruelty. *(1200)*

27. And since their endeavour toward God is good, therefore if they will still persevere and walk on still with God, he will walk on still with them. And their endeavour shall not be a void foolish thing, but a fruitful work toward the attaining of faith. *(581)*

28. Thou wilt haply say that it is not enough that a man do none evil, but he must also do good. This is

very truth that ye say. But first, if there be but these two steps to heaven, he that getteth him on the one is half up. And over that, whoso doth none evil, it will be very hard but he must needs do good, since man's mind is never so idle but occupied commonly either with good or evil. And therefore, when folk have few words and use much musing, likewise as among many words all be not always well and wisely set, so, when the tongue lieth still, if the mind be not occupied well it were less evil, save for wordly rebuke, to blabber on trifles somewhat sottishly, than while they seem sage in keeping silence, secretly peradventure the meanwhile to fantasy with themselves filthy sinful devices, whereof their tongues, if they were set on babbling, could not for shame utter and speak the like. I say not this for that I would have folks fall to babbling, well knowing, as the Scripture saith, in many words lacketh not sin, but that I would have folk in their silence take good heed that their minds he occupied with good thoughts, for unoccupied be they never. For if ever the mind were empty, it would be empty when the body sleepeth. But if it were then all empty, we should have no dreams. Then, if the fantasies leave us not sleeping, it is not likely that ever they leave us waking. Wherefore, as I say, let us keep our minds occupied with good thoughts, or else the devil will fill them with evil. *(75)*

29. To show also that God giveth not ordinarily the faith to folk but with some manner of inclination and conformity of their own good will, our Lord saith himself unto the city that he so sore longed to convert, "Jerusalem, Jerusalem, how oft have I willed to gather thy children together as an hen gathered together her chickens, and thou wouldst not" (Matt. 23, 37). No man here doubteth but that our Lord, if he would have used

some such ways as he could—it was in his power to inspire the knowledge of himself into their hearts, and of all thing that he would have them believe—and that in such wise that they could not choose but know it, and that in such wise that they could not have thought the contrary. But God had determined to bring man to salvation, not in such inevitable manner, nor without some willing conversion and turning of man toward him, though man cannot turn unto him without anticipation and concurrent help of God's especial grace. *(583)*

MARCH

1. *O blessed Saviour Jesus Christ, which willingly didst determine to die for man's sake, mollify mine hard heart and soften it so by grace, that through tender compassion of thy bitter passion I may be partner of thine holy redemption. (1290)*

2. But whoso doth, which I beseech we may all do, cast out the devil and his works by the sacrament of penance, and then in the memorial and remembrance of Christ's passion, receive that blessed sacrament with true faith and devotion with all honour and worship, as to the reverence of Christ's blessed person present in it appertaineth; they that so receive the blessed sacrament, verily receive and eat the blessed body of Christ and that not only sacramentally but also effectually, not only the figure but the thing also, not only his blessed flesh into their bodies but also his Holy Spirit into their souls, by participation whereof he is incorporate in them and they in him, and be made lively members of his mystical body the congregation of all saints of which their souls shall, if they persevere, attain the fruit and fruition clean and pure ones purged after this transitory life, and their flesh also shall Christ resuscitate into the same glory as himself hath promised. *(1076)*

3. As many a good, poor, simple unlearned soul honoureth God full devoutly under the name of God, that cannot yet tell such a tale of God as some great clerks can, that are yet for lack of like devotion, nothing near so much in God's grace and favour. *(1339)*

4. And therefore good Christian readers, would God the world were such as every man were so good, spiritual, temporal, and all, that neither part could find any fault in other and all these heresies so clean gone and forgotten and all those that are infected were so clean turned and changed, that no man needed either abjuration or punishment. But since that this is more easy to wish than likely to look for, therefore is it wisdom that spiritual and temporal both, albeit men be not all saints, yet if their conditions be tolerable, either part labour to make himself better, and charitably somewhat either part bear with other. And those extreme vices which neither the one nor the other ought in any wise to suffer, as theft, adultery, sacrilege, murder, incest, and perjury, sedition, insurrection, treason and heresy, both parts in one agreeing, to the honour of God and peace of Christ's Church, with rest, wealth, and surety of the prince and the realm, diligently reform and amend in such as are amendable, and those whose corrupt canker no cure can heal, cut off in season for corrupting farther. *(925)*

5. And albeit that I know well my wickedness hath been such that I know myself well worthy that God should let me lapse, yet can I not but trust in his merciful goodness, that as his grace hath strengthened me hitherto and made me content in my heart to lose goods, lands and life too, rather than to swear against my conscience, and hath also put in the King toward me that good and gracious mind, that as yet he hath taken from me nothing but my liberty (wherewith, as help me God, his Grace hath done me so great good by the spiritual profit that I trust I take thereby, that among all his great benefits heaped upon me so thick, I reckon upon my faith my imprisonment even the very chief) I

cannot, I say, therefore mistrust the grace of God, but that either he shall conserve and keep the King in that gracious mind still to do me none hurt, or else if his pleasure be, that for mine other sins I shall suffer in such case in sight as I shall not deserve, his grace shall give me strength to take it patiently, and peradventure somewhat gladly too, whereby his high goodness shall, by the merits of his bitter passion joined thereunto, and far surmounting in merit for me, all that I can suffer myself, make it serve for the release of my pain in Purgatory and over that for increase of some reward in heaven. Mistrust him will I not, though I feel me faint, yea, and though I should feel my fear even at point to overthrow me too, yet shall I remember how St Peter, with a blast of wind, began to sink for his faint faith, and shall do as he did, call upon Christ and pray him to help. And then I trust he shall set his holy hand unto me, and in the stormy seas hold me up from drowning. Yea, and if he suffer me to play St Peter further and to fall full to the ground and swear and forswear too, which our Lord for his tender passion keep me from, and let me lose if it so fall and never win thereby, yet after shall I trust that his goodnes will cast upon me his tender piteous eye as he did upon St Peter, and make me stand up again and confess the truth of my conscience afresh, and abide the shame and the harm here of mine own frailty. And finally, this I wot well, that without my fault he will not let me be lost. I shall therefore with good hope commit myself wholely to him. And if he suffer me for my faults to perish yet shall I then serve for a praise of his justice. But in good faith, I trust that his tender pity shall keep my poor soul safe and make me commend his mercy.
(1442)

6. And thus fareth it in the night's fear of tribulation, in which the devil, to bear down and overwhelm with dread the faithful hope that we should have in God, casteth in our imagination much more fear than cause. For while there walk in that night not only the lions' whelps but over that all the beasts of the wood beside, the beast that we hear roar in the dark night of tribulation and fear it for a lion we sometime find well afterward in the day that it was no lion at all but a foolish rude roaring ass; and the thing that on the sea seemeth sometimes a rock, is indeed nothing else but a mist. Howbeit, as the prophet saith, he that faithfully dwelleth in the hope of God's help, the shield of his truth shall so fence him round about, that be it an ass, colt, or a lion's whelp, a rock of stone or a mist, the night's fear thereof shall he nothing need to dread at all. *(1181)*

7. For as that glorious martyr holy Saint Cyprian saith, "Out of us be they all gone, and not we out of them." But ever from the beginning as heretics or schismatics have risen, either have they by profession departed out, or the Church has cast them out, and the Church evermore hath as the very flock continued still and remained, and the branches so cut off, have first or last withered away. And so shall all these at length, when the Catholic Church shall abide and remain and stand fast with God and God with it, according to God's promise, till the world take an end, and ever miracles in it, and in only it, to declare and make open that the very faith, the very hope, the very charity still continueth therein, and that how sick so ever it be, and how much dead flesh soever be found in the sick and sore parts of the same, yet alive is ever the body of this Church, for in it is the soul and the spirit, and out of the body of this known, continued Catholic

Church, there is in the body of any other Church gone
out or cast out for their contrary belief and faith, or
for their rebellious behaviour, there neither is, I say,
nor can be among them all, as all the old holy doctors
and saints fully record and testify, neither health, life,
head, nor spirit. *(659)*

8. Every faithful man knows well also that God
never teacheth against the truth, nor writeth against
his word, but that the contrariety that seemeth, ariseth
of heretics malicious subtlety, or as holy St Austin
saith, for lack of well understanding. Which misunder-
standing may soon mislead that man which chooses to
leave the faith of Christ's Catholic church and lean
to the doctrine of a false heretic, or to the liking his
own wit. *(475)*

9. So that unto all good Christian men the outward
sensible signs in all the sacraments and holy ceremonies
of Christ's church, by one general and common signification of them all, betoken and do signify and that
right effectually, an inward secret gift and inspiration
effused into the soul with the receiving of that holy
sacrament of the Holy Spirit of God. *(375)*

10. For we say that God hath made his revelations to
his church, partly by writing, partly without, and that
in these two manners the revelations of God still abide
and continue in his church, in scripture and traditions
delivered to the evangelists and apostles of Christ unto
the church, and that over that, Christ himself and his
Holy Spirit do still by secret inspiration, reveal and
open unto his Church, every necessary truth that he will
have his Church farther know and bounden to believe.
(814)

11. Let us every man therefore in time learn to love, as we should, God above all thing, and all other thing for him. And whatsoever love be not referred to that end, that is to say the pleasure of God, it is a very vain and unfruitful love. And whatsoever love we bear any creature, whereby we love God the less, that love is a loathesome love and hindereth us from heaven. For whatsoever thing we love whereby we break God's commandment, that love we better than God, and that is a love deadly and damnable. *(1306)*

12. The devil taketh his occasions as he seeth them fall meet for him. Some he stirreth to it for weariness of themself after some great loss, some for fear of horrible bodily harm, and some for fear of worldly shame. One knew I myself that had been long reputed for a right honest man, which was fallen in such a phantasy that he was well near worn away therewith. But what he was tempted to do, that would he not tell no man, but he told unto me that he was sore cumbered and that it alway ran in his mind that folk's phantasies were fallen from him, and that they esteemed not his wit as they were wont to do, but ever his mind gave him that the people began to take him for a fool. And folk, of truth, nothing so did at all, but reputed him both for wise and honest. Two other knew I that were marvellously afeared that they should kill themself, and could tell me no cause wherefore they so feared it, but only that their own mind so gave them. Neither loss had they any had, nor no such thing toward them, nor none occasion of any worldly shame; the one in body very well liking and lusty, but wondrous weary were they both twain of that mind. And alway they thought that do it they would not for nothing. And nevertheless they ever feared they should, and wherefore they so both

feared, neither of them both could tell. The devil, as I said before, seeketh his occasions. *(1195)*

13. After this, as the Duke of Norfolk and Sir Thomas More chanced to fall in familiar talk together, the Duke said unto him, "By the Mass, Master More, it is perilous striving with Princes. And therefore I would wish you somewhat to incline to the King's pleasure, for, by God's body, Master More, *Indignatio principis mors est*" (Prov. 16, 14). "Is that all, my Lord?" quoth he. "Then in faith is there no more difference between your Grace and me, but that I shall die today and you tomorrow." *(35*)*

14. And surely everything hath his mean. There is, as Scripture saith, time to speak and time to keep thy tongue. Whensoever the communication is nought and ungodly, it is better to hold thy tongue and think on some better thing the while, than to give ear thereto and support the tale. And yet better were it than holding thy tongue, properly to speak, and with some good grace and pleasant fashion to break into some better matter; by which thy speech and talking thou shalt not only profit thyself as thou shouldst have done by thy well minded silence, but also amend the whole audience, which is a thing far better and of much more merit. Howbeit, if thou can find no proper means to break the tale, except thy bare authority suffice to command silence, it were peradventure good rather to keep a good silence thyself than blunder forth rudely and irritate them to anger, which shall haply therefore not allow to talk on, but speak much the more, lest they should seem to leave at thy commandment. And better were it for the while, to let one wanton word pass uncontrolled, than give occasion of twain. But if the

communication be good, then is it better not only to give ear thereto, but also first well and prudently to devise with thyself upon the same, and then moderately and in good manner, if thou find aught to the purpose, speak thereto and say thy mind therein. *(76)*

15. The selfsame prelate had on a time made of his own drawing a certain treaty that should serve for a league between that country and a great prince. In which treaty himself thought that he had devised his articles so wisely and indited them so well that all the world would allow them. Whereupon longing sore to be praised, he called unto him a friend of his, a man well learned and of good worship and very well expert in those matters, as he that had been divers times ambassador for that country and had made many such treaties himself. When he took him the treaty and that he had read it, he asked him how he liked it and said, "But I pray you heartily tell me the very truth." And that he spake so heartily that the other had supposed he would gladly have heard the truth, and in trust thereof he told him a fault therein. At the hearing whereof he swore in great anger, "By the Mass! Thou art a very fool!" The other afterward told me that he would never tell him truth again. If they be content to hear the truth, let them then make much of those that tell them the truth, and withdraw their ear from them that falsely flatter them, and they shall be more truly served than with twenty requests praying men to tell them truth. *(1223)*

16. Therefore have we great cause with great dread and reverence to consider well the state of our own soul when we shall go to the board of God, and as near as we can (with the help of his special grace dili-

gently prayed for before) purge and cleanse our souls by confession, contrition and penance, with full purpose of forsaking from henceforth the proud desires of the devil, the greedy craving for wretched worldly wealth, and the foul passion of the filthy flesh, and be in full mind to persevere and continue in the ways of God and holy cleanness of spirit: lest that if we presume so unreverently to receive this precious stone, this pure pearl, the blessed body of our Saviour himself contained in the sacramental sign of bread, that like a sort of swine, rooting in the dirt and wallowing in the mire, we tread it under the filthy feet of our foul affections, while we set more by them than by it, intending to walk and wallow in the puddle of foul filthy sin, therewith the legion of devils may get leave of Christ to enter into us, as they got leave of him to enter into the hogs of Genesareth, and as they ran forth with them, and never stopped till they drowned them in the sea, so run on with us (but if God of his great mercy refrain them and give us the grace to repent) else not fail to drown us in the deep sea of everlasting sorrow. Of this great outrageous peril the blessed apostle St Paul giveth us gracious warning where he saith in his first epistle to the Corinthians, "Whosoever eat the body and drink the cup of our Lord unworthily, he shall be guilty of the body and blood of our Lord" (1 Cor. 11, 27). And therefore to the intent that we may avoid well this unbearable danger, and in such wise receive the body and blood of our Lord as God may of his goodness accept us for worthy, and therefore not only enter with his blessed flesh and blood sacramentally and bodily into our bodies, and also with his Holy Spirit graciously and effectually into our souls, St Paul saith, "Let a man prove himself and so eat of that bread and drink of that cup" (1 Cor. 11, 28). But then in what wise shall we prove ourselves? We may not go rashly to God's board, but by a convenient time taken before. We must, as I began to say, consider well and examine surely what state our soul standeth in. In which thing it will be not only right hard, but also peradventure impossible, by any possible diligence of ourselves to attain unto the very full undoubted surety thereof without special revelation of God. But God yet in this point is of his high goodness content if we do the diligence that we can, to see that we be not in the purpose of any deadly sin. *(1265)*

17. *Give me thy grace to amend my life, and to have an eye to mine end without grudge of death, which to them that die in thee, good Lord, is the gate of a wealthy life. (1417)*

18. But now, while we well know that there is no king so great, but that all the while he walketh here, walk he never so loose, ride he with never so strong an army for his defence, yet himself is very sure though he seek in the mean season some other pastime to put it out of his mind—yet is he very sure, I say, that escape can he not; and very well he knoweth that he hath already sentence given upon him to die, and that verily die he shall, and that himself, though he hope upon respite of his execution, yet can he not tell how soon. And therefore, but if he be a fool, he can never be without fear that either on the morrow, or on the selfsame day, the grisly, cruel hangman death, which from his first coming in hath ever hovered aloof and looked toward him, and ever lain in await on him, shall amidmong all his royalty, and all his main strength, neither kneel before him nor make him any reverence, nor with any good manner desire him to come forth,

but rigorously and fiercely grip him by the very breast and make all his bones rattle, and so, by long and divers sore torments, strike him stark dead in this prison, and then cause his body to be cast into the ground in a foul pit, within some corner of the same, there to rot and be eaten with wretched worms of the earth, sending yet his soul out farther unto a more fearful judgment, whereof at his temporal death his success is uncertain, and therefcre, though, by God's grace, not out of good hope, yet for all that, in the meanwhile, in very sore dread and fear, and peradventure in peril inevitable of eternal fire, too. *(1244)*

19. For if a fornicator dispraise lechery and commend chastity, or the proud preach against pride and praise humility, or the covetous wretch rebuke avarice and laud liberality, the glutton discommend gluttony and exhort all men to abstinence, and so forth in such other like, though these words seem unfitting in such men's mouths, yet may he that listeth well to consider therein the great strength of truth and of virtue, which expresseth his own praise out of the mouth of his enemy, and him that taketh shame thereby and holdeth a torch light and bright burning in his own hand to let the people the better behold his faults, and the more to wonder on himself in honour of the truth. *(704)*

20. For men use, if they have an evil turn, to write it in marble; and whoso doth us a good turn, we write it in dust. *(57)*

21. But the gospels and Holy Scripture God provideth that though maybe some of it may perish and be lost, whereby they might have harm but not fall in error—for the faith should stand though the Scriptures

were all gone—yet shall he never suffer his Church to be deceived in that point that they shall take for Holy Scripture any book that is not. And therefore saith holy St Austin, "I should not believe the gospel, but if it were for the Church." And he saith for good reason. For were it not for the Spirit of God keeping the truth thereof in his Church, who could be sure which were the very gospels? There were many that wrote the gospel. And yet hath the Church by secret instruct of God, rejected the remnant and chosen out these four for the sure undoubted truth. *(175)*

22. Now are the affections of men's minds imprinted by divers means. One way, by the mean of the bodily senses moved by such things, pleasant or displeasant, as are outwardly through sensible worldly things offered and objected unto them. And this manner of receiving the impression of affections is common unto men and beasts. Another manner of receiving affections is by the mean of reason, which both ordinately tempereth those affections, that the bodily five wits imprint, and also disposeth a man many times to some spiritual virtues, very contrary to those affections that are fleshly and sensual. And those reasonable dispositions be affections spiritual and proper to the nature of man, and above the nature of beasts. Now as our spiritual enemy the devil enforceth himself to make us lean unto the sensual affections and beastly, so doth Almighty God of his goodness by his Holy Spirit inspire us good motions, with aid and help of his grace, toward the other affections spiritual, and by sundry means instructeth our reason to lean unto them, and not only to receive them as engendred and planted in our soul, but also in such wise water them with the wise advertisement of godly counsel and continual prayer, that they may be habitual-

ly radicate and surely take deep root therein. And after as the one kind of affection or the other beareth the strength in our heart, so be we stronger or feebler against the terror of death in this cause. *(1249)*

23. A scolding wife once told her husband when she came from confession, "Be merry, man," quoth she, "for this day I thank God was I well shriven, and I purpose now therefore to leave off all mine old nagging and begin even afresh." It seemed she spake it half in sport. For that she said she would cast away all her nagging, therein, I suppose she sported; but in that she said she would begin it all afresh, her husband found that good earnest. *(1184)*

24. I cannot liken my life more meetly now than to the snuff of a candle that burneth within the candle-stick's nose. For as the snuff sometimes burneth down so low, that whoso looketh on it would ween it were quite out, and yet suddenly lifteth up a flame half an inch above the nose and giveth a pretty short light again, and thus playeth divers times, till at last ere it be looked for out it goeth altogether; so have I divers such days together, as every day of them I look even for to die. And yet have I then after that some such few days again in which a man would think that I might yet well continue. But I know my lingering not likely to last long, but out will my snuff suddenly some day within a while, and therefore will I with God's help, seem never so well amended, nevertheless reckon every day for my last. For though that to the repressing of the bold courage of blind youth, there is a very true proverb, that as soon cometh a young sheep's skin to the market as an old; yet this difference there is at least between them, that as the young man may happen

sometime to die soon, so the old man can never live long. *(1172)*

25. This Catholic known church is that mystical body be it never so sick whereof the principal head is Christ. Of which body, whether the successor of St Peter be his vicar-general and head under him, as all Christian nations have long taken him, is no part of this question. For to this matter it is enough that this body mystical of Christ, this Catholic Church, is that body that is animated, hath life spiritual, and is inspired with the Holy Spirit of God that maketh them of one faith in the house of God by leading them into the consent of every necessary truth of revealed faith, be they in conditions and manners never so like, as long as they be conformable and content in the unity of faith to cleave unto that body. Of this church can we not be deceived, nor of the right faith can we not be deceived while we cleave to this Church since this Church is it into which God hath given his spirit of faith, and in this Church both good and bad profess one faith. For if any profess the contrary faith, be it any one man or any one country, they be checked, noted and reproved by the whole body and soon knowen from the body. *(528)*

26. Many a good man there is which without force at all, or any necessity wherefore he should so do, suffereth these two things (to have less room to walk in, or to have the door shut upon us) willingly of his own choice with much hardness more—holy monks, I mean, of the Charterhouse order, such as never pass their cells, but only to the church set fast by their cells, and thence to their cells again; and St Bridget's order; and St Clare's much like, and, in a manner all close religious houses. And yet anchorites and an-

choresses most specially, all whose whole room is less than a moderately large chamber; and yet are they there as well content many long years together, as are other men, and better men too, that walk about the world. And therefore you may see that the loathness of less room and the door shut upon us, while so many folk are so well content therewith, and will for God's love live so to choose, is but an horror enhanced of their own phantasy. *(1247)*

27. Now doth God with his Christian folks ordinarily take that way in the giving them their belief and faith, that though they do not merit with any forgoing good deeds, nor deserve the gift of believing, yet may they with good endeavour and obedient conformity deserve and merit in the believing. *(582)*

28. As for fame and glory desired but for worldly pleasure, doth unto the soul inestimable harm. For that setteth men's hearts upon high devices and desires of such things as are immoderate and outrageous, and by help of false flatteries puff up a man in pride, and make a mortal man lately made of earth, and that shall again shortly be laid full low in earth, and there lie and rot and turn again into earth, take himself in the meantime for a god here upon earth, and think to win himself to be lord of all the earth. *(1226)*

29. But it may be that as men be changeable, he that is predestinate may be many times in his life nought. And he that will at last fall to sin and wretchedness and so finally cast himself away, shall in some time of his life be good and therefore for a time in God's favour. For God blameth nor hateth no man for that he shall will but for that malicious will that he hath or hath had already. *(182)*

30. For it is not sin to have riches, but to love riches. "If riches come to you, set not your heart thereon, (Ps. 61, 10)" saith Holy Scripture. He that setteth not his heart thereon, nor casteth not his love thereon, reckoneth, as it is indeed, himself not the richer by them, nor those goods not his own, but delivered him by God to be faithfully disposed upon himself and others, and that of the disposition he must give the reckoning. And therefore, as he reckoneth himself never the richer, so is he never the prouder. But he that forgetteth his goods to be the goods of God, and of a disposer reckoneth himself an owner, he taketh himself for rich. And because he reckoneth the riches his own, he casteth a love thereto, and so much is his love the less set unto God. For as Holy Scripture saith, "Where thy treasure is, there is thine heart" (Matt. 6, 21); where if thou didst reckon the treasure not thine, but the treasure of God delivered thee to dispose and bestow, thy treasure should be in earth and thy heart in heaven. But these covetous folk that set their hearts on their hoards and be proud when they look on their heaps, they reckon themselves rich and be indeed very wretched beggars; those I mean that be full christened in covetousness, that have all the properties belonging to the name, that is to wit, that be as loath to spend aught as they be glad to get all. For they not only part nothing liberally with other folk, but also live wretchedly by sparing from themselves. And so they reckon themselves owners, and be indeed but the bare keepers of other men's goods. For since they find in their heart to spend nothing upon themselves, but keep all for their executors, they make it even now not their own while they use it not but other men's for whose use and benefit they keep it. *(92)*

31. Christ will have you believe all that he telleth you, and do all that he biddeth you, and forbear all that he forbiddeth you, without any manner exception. Break one of his commandments, and break all. Forsake one point of his faith, and forsake all, as for any thanks you get of him for the remnant. And therefore if you devise as it were indentures between God and you, what thing you will do for him and what thing you will not do, as though he should hold him content with such service of yours as yourself please to appoint him; if you make, I say, such indentures, you shall seal both the parts yourself and you get thereto none agreement of him. *(1228)*

APRIL

1. *Good Lord, give us thy grace not to read or hear this Gospel of thy bitter passion with our eyes and our ears in manner of a pastime, but that it may with compassion so sink into our hearts that it may stretch to the everlasting profit of our souls. (1292)*

2. For this we may be sure, that whoso dishonour God in one place with occasion of a false faith, all honour that he doeth him anywhere beside, is odious and despiteful and rejected of God and never shall save that faithless soul from the fire of hell. From which our Lord give them grace truly to turn in time, so that we and they together in one Catholic Church, knit with God together in one Catholic faith, faith I say, not faith alone as they do, but accompanied with good hope and with her chief sister well working charity, may so receive Christ's blessed sacraments here, and especially that we may receive himself, his very blessed body, very flesh and blood, in the blessed sacrament, our holy blessed housel, that we may here be with him incorporate so by grace, that after the short course of this transitory life, with his tender pity poured upon us in purgatory, at the prayer of good people, and intercession of holy saints, we may be with them in their holy fellowship incorporate in Christ in his eternal glory. Amen. *(1138)*

3. Needs must the man take little fruit of the Scripture if he either believe not that it were the word of God, or else think that, though it were, it might for all that be untrue. This faith, as it is more faint or more

strong, so shall the comfortable words of Holy Scripture stand the man in more stead or less. *(1143)*

4. If we would not suffer the strength and fervour of our faith to wax lukewarm, or rather key-cold, and in manner lose his vigour by scattering our minds abroad about so many trifling things, that of the matters of our faith we very seldom think, but that we would withdraw our thought from the respect and regard of all worldly fantasies, and so gather our faith together into a little narrow room, and like the little grain of mustard seed which is of nature hot, set it in the garden of our soul, all weeds pulled out, for the better feeding of our faith; then shall it grow, and so spread up in height, that the birds, that is to wit, the holy angels of heaven, shall breed in our soul and bring forth virtues in the branches of our faith. *(1143)*

5. For God doth reveal his truths not always in one manner but sometime he showeth it out at once as he will have it known and men bounden forthwith to believe it, as he showed Moses what he would have Pharaoh do. Sometime he sheweth it leisurely, suffering his flock to come and dispute thereupon, and in their treating of the matter, suffereth them with good mind and Scripture and natural wisdom with invocation of his spiritual help, to search and seek for the truth, and to vary for the while in their opinions, till that he reward their virtuous diligence with leading them secretly into the consent and concord and belief of the truth of his Holy Spirit which maketh his flock of one mind in his house, that is to say his Church. *(456)*

6. If the Spirit of God governing the Church and leading it into all truth, put us not in surety and cer-

tainty of the truth, how could he be to us as he is named *paracletus*, that is comforter, if we were left so comfortless that we were uncertain whether the whole Church were in damnable error instead of the right faith? *(503)*

7. If man's will had no more part toward the attaining of the belief than the child hath in the begetting of his own father, I see not wherefore our Saviour should call upon the people and bid them do penance and believe the Gospel as he doth in the first chapter of St Mark. For though it be very true that, without God's help and God's grace predisposing and foregoing, no man can believe, yet if there were nothing in the man himself whereby he might receive it, if he would with grace, which God of his goodness offereth, apply himself towardly to the receiving thereof, and whereby on the other side, he might perversely refuse it, or of sloth and negligence so slightly regard it that he were worthy to lose it—if there were, I say, no such thing in the man whereby he himself might somewhat do therein with God, our Lord would not call upon men and exhort them to believe, and praise them that will believe and rebuke them that will not believe as he doth in many places of the Scripture. *(580)*

8. Truth is it that the passion of Christ and offering up of himself unto his Father upon the cross, is a satisfaction for the sin of all that repent, as that we repent aright and effectually, by confession, by contrition and by penitential deeds, revenging our sins upon ourself, with good works of charity, the more largely increased towards our neighbours doing fruitful penance, bringing forth the fruits of penance and according to the counsel of St John Baptist, not slight fruits,

simple and single, but fruits good, great and worthy, and yet not of themselves worthy, but such as the satisfaction of Christ maketh worthy, without which we could nothing satisfy, but with which we may, since his pleasure is that we so should, and not so take his death for so full satisfaction of altogether that we should therefore be careless and slothful to do any penance ourself for our own sin. *(533)*

9. The common articles of faith be requisite to be had of every man before he meddle with the reading of the Scripture. For if he shall without knowledge had of them before and without firm credence given to them before, go seek them out in the Scripture, he shall both be long ere he get them, and shall also stand in great peril to fall into the contrary heresies, as other heretics have done before. *(818)*

10. Think not that everything is pleasant that men for madness laugh at. For thou shalt in Bedlam see one laugh at the knocking of his own head against a post, and yet there is little pleasure therein. But ye think perchance this example as mad as the mad man, and as little to the purpose. I am content ye so think. But what will ye say if ye see men that are taken and reputed wise laugh much more madly than he? Shall ye not see such laugh at their own craft when they have, as they think, wilfully done their neighbour wrong? Now whoso seeth not that his laughter is more mad than the laughter of the mad man, I hold him madder than they both. For the mad man laughed when he had done himself but little hurt by a knock of his head to a post. This other sage fool laugheth at the casting of his own soul into the fire of hell, for which he hath cause to weep all his life. And it cannot be but the fear thereof followeth

his laughter, and secret sorrow marreth all such outward mirth. For the heart of a wicked wretch is like a stormy sea that cannot rest, except a man be fallen down into the dungeon of wretchedness and the door shut over his head. For when a sinner is once fallen down into the depth, he becometh a desperate wretch and setteth all at nought, and he is in the worst kind of all and farthest from all recovery. For like as in the body his sickness is most incurable that is sick and feeleth it not, but thinketh himself whole (for he that is in that case is commonly mad) so he that by a mischievous custom of sin perceiveth no fault in his evil deed nor hath no remorse thereof, hath lost the natural light of reason and the spiritual light of faith, which two lights of knowledge and understanding quenched, what remaineth in him more than the bodily senses and sensual wits common to man and brute beasts? *(73)*

11. Why lovest thou so this brittle world's joy?
Take all the mirth, take all the fantasies,
Take every game, take every wanton toy,
Take every sport that men can thee devise:
And among them all on warrantise
Thou shalt no pleasure comparable find
To th'inward gladness of a virtuous mind. *(26)*

12. For we, beside the Scripture, do believe the Church because that God himself by secret inspiration of his Holy Spirit doth, if we be willing to learn, teach us to believe his Church. And also, if we will walk with him, leadeth us into the belief thereof by the self-same mean by which he teacheth us and leadeth us in to the belief of his Holy Scripture. For likewise as when we hear the Scripture or read it, if we be not rebellious but endeavour ourself to believe, and captive and subdue

our understanding to serve and follow faith, praying for his gracious aid and help, he then worketh with us and inwardly doth incline our heart into the assent of that we read, and, after a little spark of our faith, increaseth the credence in our incredulity. So doth his goodness in likewise incline and move the mind of every like toward and like well-willing body to the giving of fast and firm credence to the faith that the Church teacheth him in such things as be not in Scripture, and to believe that God hath taught his Church those points by his holy word without writing. *(206)*

13. Many things every man learned knows well there are in which every man is at liberty without peril of damnation to think which way him please till the one part be determined for necessary to be believed by a general council and I am not he that take upon me to define or determine of what kind or nature everything is that the oath containeth, nor am so bold or presumptuous to blame or dispraise the conscience of other men, their truth nor their learning neither, nor I meddle with no man but of myself, nor of no man's conscience else will I meddle but of mine own. And in mine own conscience I cry God mercy, I find of mine own life matters enough to think on. I have lived, methinks, a long life and now neither I look nor I long to live much longer. I have since I came in the Tower looked once or twice to have given up my spirit ere this and in good faith mine heart grew the lighter with hope thereof. Yet forget I not that I have a long reckoning and a great to give account of, but I put my trust in God and in the merits of his bitter passion, and I beseech him give me and keep me the mind to long to be out of this world and to be with him. For I can never but trust that who so long to be with him shall be welcome to him and

on the other side my mind giveth me verily that any that ever shall come to him shall full heartily wish to be with him or ever he shall come at him. *(1444)*

14. St Thomas of Inde, after he had both seen him [Our Lord] and felt him, did by sight and feeling know his manhood, and therewith by faith believed his godhead; even so we know the Church by sight, hearing and feeling, as we know drapers and mercers. And we believe the spirit of God abiding therewith and leading it into all truth, and Christ the chief head thereof assisting it and preserving it from failing against all the gates of hell. And we believe that it is but one Church by profession of baptism, holily dedicated unto God. *(804)*

15. So surely if we custom ourself to put our trust of comfort in the delight of these peevish worldly things, God shall for that foul fault suffer our tribulation to grow so great that all the pleasures of this world shall never bear us up, but all our peevish pleasure shall in the depth of tribulation drown with us. *(1144)*

16. In this proving and examination of ourself which St Paul speaketh of, one very special point must be to prove and examine ourself and see that we be in right faith and belief concerning the holy blessed sacrament itself. That is to say, that we verily believe that it is, as in deed it is, under the form and likeness of bread, the very blessed body, flesh, and blood of our holy Saviour Christ himself, the very self same body, and the very self same blood, that died and was shed upon the cross for our sin, and the third day gloriously did arise again to life and, with the souls of holy saints fetched out of hell, ascended and rose up wonderfully into heaven and there sitteth on the right hand of the Father, and shall

visibly descend in great glory to judge the quick and the dead, and reward all men after their works. *(1266)*

17. *Good Lord, give me the grace, in all my fear and agony, to have recourse to that great fear and wonderful agony that thou my sweet Saviour, hadst at the Mount of Olivet before thy most bitter passion, and in the meditation thereof, to conceive spiritual comfort and consolation profitable for my soul. (1417)*

18. I believe, Meg, that they that put me here [the Tower] imagine they have done me a high displeasure. But I assure thee, on my faith, my own good daughter, if it had not been for my wife and you that be my children, whom I account the chief part of my charge, I would not have failed long ere this to have closed myself in as strait a room and straiter too. But since I am come hither without mine own desert, I trust that God of his goodness will discharge me of my care, and with his gracious help supply my lack among you. I find no cause, I thank God, Meg, to reckon myself in worse case here than in my own house. For me thinketh God maketh me a wanton and setteth me on his lap and dandleth me. *(37★)*

19. And therefore, like as I would advise every man in every sickness of the body, to be shriven and seek of a good spiritual physician the sure health of his soul, which shall not only serve against peril that may peradventure farther grow by that sickness than in the beginning men would think were likely; but the comfort thereof and God's favour increasing therewith, shall also do the body good (for which cause the blessed apostle St James exhorteth men that they shall in their bodily sickness induce the priests and saith it shall do them good both in body and soul) so would I sometime

advise some men in some sickness of the soul, beside
their spiritual healer, take some counsel of the physician
for the body. *(1196)*

20. Daughter Margaret, we two have talked of this
thing ofter than twice or thrice, and that same tale
in effect that you tell me now therein, and the same
fear too, have you twice told me before, and I have twice
answered you too, that in this matter if it were possible
for me to do the thing that might content the King's
Grace, and God therewith not offended, there hath no
man taken this oath already more gladly than I would
do; as he that reckoneth himself more deeply bounden
unto the King's Highness for his most singular bounty,
many ways showed and declared, than any of them all
beside. But since standing my conscience, I can no
wise do it, and that for the instruction of my conscience in the matter, I have not slightly looked, but by
many years studied and advisedly considered, and never
could yet see nor hear that thing, nor I think I never
shall, that could induce mine own mind to think otherwise than I do, I have no manner remedy, but God
hath given me to the straight, that either I must deadly
displease him, or abide any worldly harm that he shall
for mine other sins, under name of this thing, suffer
to fall upon me. Whereof, as I before this have told
you too, I have ere I came here [the Tower] not left
unbethought nor unconsidered, the very worst and the
uttermost that can by possibility fall. And albeit that
I know mine own frailty full well and the natural
faintness of mine own heart, yet if I had not trusted
that God should give me strength rather to endure all
things, than offend him by swearing ungodly against
mine own conscience, you may be very sure I would
not have come here. And since I look in this matter

but only unto God, it maketh me little matter, though
man call it as it pleaseth them and say it is no conscience but a foolish scruple. *(1434)*

21. Let us here now, good readers, before we proceed
farther, consider well this matter and ponder well this
fearful point, what horrible peril there is in that persis-
tent sin of pride, what abominable sin it is in the sight of
God, when any creature falleth into the delight and
liking of itself; as the thing whereupon continued,
inevitably faileth not to follow, first the neglecting, and
after that contemning and finally, with disobedience
and rebellion, the very full forsaking of God. *(1272)*

22. Think ye not now that it will be a gentle pleasure,
when we lie dying, all our body in pain, all our mind in
trouble, our soul in sorrow, our heart all in dread while
our life walketh awayward, while our breath draweth
toward, while the devil is busy about us, while we lack
stomach and strength to bear any one of so manifold
heinous troubles, will it not be, as I was about to say, a
pleasant thing to see before thine eyes and hear at thine
ear a rabble of fleshly friends, or rather of flesh flies,
skipping about thy bed and thy sick body, like ravens
about thy corpse, now almost carrion, crying to thee
on every side, "What shall I have? What shall I have?"
Then shall come thy children and cry for their parts;
then shall come thy sweet wife, and where in thine
health perhaps she spake thee not one sweet word in
six weeks, now shall she call thee sweet husband and
weep with much work and ask thee what shall she
have; then shall thine executors ask for the keys, and
ask what money is owing thee, ask what substance thou
hast, and ask where thy money lieth. And while thou
liest in that case, their words shall be so tedious that

thou wilt wish all that they ask for upon a red fire, so thou mightest lie one half-hour in rest. *(78)*

23. I forgot not in this matter the counsel of Christ in the Gospel, that ere I should begin to build this castle for the safeguard of mine own soul, I should sit and reckon what the charge would be. I counted full surely many a restless night, while my wife slept, and thought that I had slept too, what peril was possible for to fall to me, so far forth that I am sure there can come none above. And in devising thereupon, I had a full heavy heart. But yet, I thank our Lord, for all that I never thought to change though the very uttermost should happen to me that my fear ran upon. *(1440)*

24. Yet God, when man hath put him out of his dwelling, doth of his great goodness, not always leave him for his unkindness, but though if the man die ere God come in again, God shall of justice for his unkindness condemn him, yet he hovereth still about the door of his heart, always knocking upon him to be by the free will of man let in with his grace into the house of man's heart again. *(540)*

25. The points of the faith are not I say in such wise showed, nor the wit in them so thoroughly so clearly instructed, but that the thing which in the wit lacketh and remaineth imperfect, may by the will be perfected and made up, and instead of sure and certain sight, be from distrust or doubtful opinion brought by God working with man's will into sure faith and undoubted belief. *(583)*

26. A like learned priest throughout all the Gospels scraped out *diabolus* and wrote *Jesus Christus* because he thought the devil's name was not meet to stand in so good a place. *(421)*

27. Where the kinds of tribulation are so divers, some of these tribulations a man may pray God take from him, and take some comfort in the trust that God will so do. And therefore against hunger, sickness, and bodily hurt, and against the loss of either body or soul, men may lawfully many times pray to the goodness of God either for themself or their friend. And towards this purpose are expressly prayed many devout orisons in the common service of our Mother Holy Church. And toward our help in some of these things serve some of the petitions in the *Pater noster*, wherein we pray daily for our daily food and to be preserved from the fall in temptation and to be delivered from evil. But yet may we not alway pray for the taking away from us of every kind of temptation. For if a man should in every sickness pray for his health again, when should he show himself content to die and to depart unto God? And that mind must a man have, ye know well, or else it will not be well. *(1146)*

28. If thy heart were indeed out of this world and in heaven, all the kinds of torment that all this world could devise, could put thee to no pain here. *(1233)*

29. Since his desire is good and declareth unto himself that he hath in God a good faith, it is a good token unto him that he is not an outcast from God's gracious favour, while he perceiveth that God hath put such a virtuous well ordered appetite in his mind. For as every evil mind cometh of the world and ourself and the devil, so is every such good mind either immediately, or by the mean of our good angel, or other gracious occasion, inspired into man's heart by the goodness of God himself. And what a comfort then may this be unto us, when we by that desire perceive a sure

undoubted token that toward our final salvation our Saviour is himself so graciously busy about us. *(1145)*

30. Consider the well-converted thief that hung on Christ's right hand. Did not he, by his meek sufferance and humble knowledge of his own fault, asking forgiveness of God and yet content to suffer for his sin, make of his just punishment and well-deserved tribulation a very good special medicine to cure him of all pain in the other world, and win him eternal salvation? *(1148)*

MAY

1. *Good Lord, which upon the sacrifice of the paschal lamb didst so clearly destroy the first-begotten children of the Egyptians, that Pharaoh was thereby forced to let the children of Israel depart out of his bondage, I beseech thee give me the grace in such faithful manner to receive the sweet paschal lamb, the very blessed body of our sweet Saviour thy son, that, the first suggestions of sin by thy power killed in my heart, I may safe depart out of the danger of the most cruel Pharaoh the devil. (1298)*

2. And if it be odious in the sight of God, that a woman beautiful indeed abuse the pride of her beauty to the vain glory of herself, how delectable is that dainty damsel to the devil that standeth in her own light and taketh herself for fair deeming herself well liked for her broad forehead, while the young man that beholdeth her, marketh more her crooked nose. *(1272)*

3. Let us never ask of God precisely our own ease by delivery from our tribulation, but pray for his aid and comfort by which ways himself shall best like, and then may we take comfort, even of our such request. For both be we sure that this mind cometh of God, and also be we very sure that as he beginneth to work with us, so, but if ourself flit from him, he will not fail to tarry with us; and then, he dwelling with us, what trouble can do us harm? "If God be with us," saith St Paul, "who can stand against us?" *(1147)*

4. Lo, dost thou not see, Meg, that these blessed fathers [the Carthusians and others] be now as cheerfully

going to their deaths as bridegrooms to their marriage? Wherefore mayest thou see, mine own good daughter, what a great difference there is between such as have in effect spent their days in a straight, hard, penitential and painful life religiously, and such as have in the world, like worldly wretches, as thy poor father hath done, consumed all their time in pleasure and ease licentiously. For God, considering their long continued life in most sore and grievous penance, will no longer suffer them to remain here in this vale of misery and iniquity, but speedily hence taketh them to the fruition of his everlasting deity, whereas thy silly father, Meg, that like a most wicked caitiff hath passed forth the whole course of his miserable life most sinfully, God, thinking him not worthy so soon to come to that eternal felicity, leaveth him here yet still in the world, further to be plunged and turmoiled with misery. *(39*)*

5. For the salvation of our soul may we boldly pray; for grace may we boldly pray; for faith, for hope, and for charity, and for every such virtue as shall serve us to heaven-ward. But as for all other things before remembered in which is contained the matter of every kind of tribulation, we may never well make prayers so precisely but that we must express or imply a condition therein; that is to wit, that if God see the contrary better for us, we refer it whole to his will, and instead of our grief taking away, pray that God may send us of his goodness either spiritual comfort to take it gladly, or strength at the least wise to bear it patiently. *(1146)*

6. Now then, if reason alone be sufficient to move a man to take pain for the gaining of worldly rest or pleasure, and for the avoiding of another pain, though

peradventure more, yet endurable but for a short season; why should not reason grounded upon the sure foundation of faith, and helped also forward with the aid of God's grace, as it ever is undoubtedly when folk for a good mind in God's name come together thereon, why should not then reason, I say, thus furthered with faith and grace, be much more able first to engender in us such an affection, and after by long and deep meditation thereof, so to continue that affection, that it shall turn into an habitual fast and deep-rooted purpose of patient suffering the painful death of this body here in earth, for the gaining of everlasting wealthy life in heaven, and avoiding of everlasting painful death in hell? *(1253)*

7. There is in this world set up as it were a game of wrestling, wherein the people of God come in on the one side, and on the other side come mighty strong wrestlers and wily, that is, to wit, the devils, the cursed proud damned spirits. For it is not our flesh alone that we must wrestle with but with the devil too. "Our wrestling is not here", saith St Paul, "against flesh and blood, but against the princes and potentates of these dark regions, against the spiritual wicked ghosts of the air" (Eph. 6, 12). But as God unto them that on his part give his adversary the fall hath prepared a crown, so he that will not wrestle shall have none. For as St Paul saith, "There shall no man have the crown but he that doth his devoir therefor according to the law of the game" (2 Tim. 2, 5). And then as holy St. Bernard saith: "How canst thou fight or wrestle therefor if there were no challenger against thee that would provoke thee thereunto?" And, therefore, may it be a great comfort, as St James saith, to every man that feeleth himself challenged and provoked by temptation; for thereby perceiveth he that it cometh to his course to

wrestle, which shall be, but if he willingly will play the coward of the fool, the matter of his eternal reward in heaven (James, I, 2-4, 12). *(1178)*

8. Albeit that God may cure a sore without a medicine, and do a miracle in a man's health, and that for the regard of the man's good faith and his trust in God, yet if it please God to heal him by a plaster though his faith be the cause why God doth it, yet is the plaster a means in the doing and serveth not for a bare sign. And surely when our Saviour set this order therein, that who so were baptized in water in the name of the Father and the Son and the Holy Ghost he should be saved, and that except a man were born again as well of the water as of the spirit, he should not enter into the kingdom of heaven, God set it to serve for a more effectual thing than for a bare sign void of any fruitful effect. For this were as if a lord would say to a poor fellow, "Take thee this livery gown of mine and if thou take it and wear it, I will take ye for mine household servant and in mine household give thee meat and drink and wages, or else if thou wear it not, thou shalt not come within my doors." This livery gown giveth him neither meat nor money, but yet it is more than a sign that he shall have it, for the wearing thereof helpeth him to get it, not of any nature of the livery but by his lord's ordinance. And so likewise though it were true that the sacraments did nothing work in themself, nor had no power in themself no more of God than of nature to purge and cleanse the soul, yet were it more than a bare token or sign of grace, in that it hath by God's promise his own special assistance, which at the sacraments ministered doth infuse his grace. *(384)*

9. He then that by fast faith and sure hope dwelleth

in God's help, and hangeth always thereupon, never
falling from that hope, he shall, saith the prophet, ever
dwell and abide in God's defence and protection; that
is to say, that while he faileth not to believe well and
hope well, God will never fail in all temptation to defend
him (Ps. 90). *(1179)*

10. I will advise you therefore good readers for the
true taking of the old faith and for the discerning thereof
from all new, to stand to the common well known belief
of the common known Catholic Church of all Christian
people such faith as by yourself and your fathers and
your grandfathers you have known to be believed and
have over that heard by them that the contrary was in
the times of their fathers and their grandfathers also
taken ever more for heresy. And also ye that read but
even in English books shall in many things perceive
the same by stories five times as far afore that. We must
also for the perceiving of the old faith from the new,
stand to the writings of the old holy doctors and saints
by whose expositions we see what points are expressed
in the Scripture and what points the Catholic Church of
Christ hath beside the Scripture received and kept by
the Spirit of God and tradition of his apostles. And
specially must we also stand in this matter of faith to
the determinations of Christ's Catholic Church. *(925)*

11. For likewise as while a man sitteth by the fire he
cannot be a-cold because the fire is by him that keepeth
him warm, so while the seed of God is in the man he
cannot sin, because the seed of God being in him doth
keep and preserve him from sin. But likewise as the
broach-turner that sitteth warm by the fire, may let
the spit stand and suffer the meat to burn and walk
himself out in the snow until his teeth chatter in his

head for cold and never catch heat again and fall stark
dead on the ground, so he that is once God's child and
hath the seed of God in him, and therefore cannot sin
deadly as long as he keepeth it and cleaveth fast unto it,
may by the folly and forwardness of his own free will
expel the seed of God and reject his grace and neglect
his Holy Spirit and fall to deadly sin and continue
therein and die therein and go to the devil therein too.
(549)

12. One of the most special things to move us to
contempt of this world and to regard much the world
to come, is to consider that in that world we shall be
for ever at home, and that in this world we be but
wayfaring folk. *(1313)*

13. So blind is our mortality and so unaware what
will fall, so unsure also what manner mind we will
ourself have tomorrow, that God could not lightly do
man a more vengeance than in this world to grant him
his own foolish wishes. *(1147)*

14. If the devil catch a man fast at the time of his
death, he is sure to keep him for ever. For as the Scripture saith, "Wheresoever the stone falleth, there shall
it abide" (Eccles. 11, 3). And since he knoweth this for
very surety and is of malice so venomous and envious
that he had rather double his own pain than suffer us
to escape from pain, he, when we draw to death, doth
his uttermost endeavour to bring us to damnation,
never ceasing to minister, by subtle and unthinkable
means, first unlawful longing to live and horror to go
gladly to God at his calling. Then giveth he some false
hope of escaping that sickness, and thereby putteth in
our mind a love yet and cleaving to the world keeping

of our goods, loathsomeness of confession, sloth towards good works. And if we be so far gone that we see we cannot recover, then he casteth in our minds presumption and security of salvation as a thing well won by our own works, of which, if we have any done well, he casteth them into our minds with over great liking and thereby withdraweth us from the haste of doing any more, as a thing that either needeth not or may be done by our executors. *(79)*

15. Let us have our sure hope in him and then shall we be very sure that we shall not be deceived. For either shall we have the thing that we hope for or a better thing in the stead. For as for the thing that we pray for, and hope to have, God will not alway send us. And therefore in all things save only for heaven, our prayer nor our hope may never be too precise, although the thing be lawful to require *(1213)*.

16. We must, I say, see that we firmly believe that this blessed sacrament is not a bare sign or a figure or a token of that holy body of Christ, but that it is, in perpetual remembrance of his bitter passion that he suffered for us, the self same precious body of Christ that suffered it, by his own almighty power and unspeakable goodness consecrated and given to us. And this point of belief is, in the receiving of this blessed sacrament of such necessity and such weight with them that have years and discretion, that without it they receive it plainly to their damnation. And that point believed very full and firmly must needs be a great occasion to move any man in all other points to receive it well. For note well the words of St Paul therein : "He that eateth of this bread and drinketh of this cup unworthily, eateth and drinketh judgement upon him-

self in that he discerneth not the body of our Lord"
(1 Cor. 11, 27). Lo! here this blessed apostle well
declareth that he which in any wise unworthily receiveth this most excellent sacrament receiveth it unto
his own damnation, in that he well declareth by his
evil demeanour towards it, in his unworthy receiving of
it, that he discerneth it not, nor judgeth it, nor taketh it
for the very body of our Lord, as in deed it is. And verily
it is hard but that this point, deeply rooted in our
breast should set all our heart in a fervour of devotion
towards the worthy receiving of that blessed body. For
surely there can be no doubt on the other side, but that
if any man believe that it is Christ's very body, and yet
is not inflamed to receive him devoutly thereby, that
man were likely to receive this blessed sacrament very
coldly and far from all devotion, if he believed that it
were not this body but only a bare token of him instead of his body. *(1266)*

17. *Almighty God, take from me all vain-glorious
minds, all appetites of mine own praise, all envy, covetousness, gluttony, sloth and evil lust, all wrathful passions, all
appetite of revenging, all desire or delight of other folks'
harm, all pleasure in provoking any person to wrath and
anger, all delight of upbraiding or insulting against any
person in their affliction and calamity. And give me,
good Lord, an humble, lowly, quiet, peaceable, patient,
charitable, kind, tender, and pitiful mind, with all my
works, and all my words, and all my thoughts, to have a
taste of thy holy, blessed Spirit. (1417)*

18. The Church therefore must needs be the common known multitude of Christian men, good and bad
together, while the Church is here in earth. For this
net of Christ hath for the while good fishes and bad.

And this field of Christ beareth for the while good corn and cockle, till it shall at the day of doom be purified, and all the bad cast out, and the only good remain. Christ himself said to his apostles, "Now be you clean, but not all" (John 13, 10), and yet were they all of his Church. Albeit that one of them was, as our Saviour said himself, a devil. "Did I not," said he, "choose twelve of you and one of you is a devil?" (John 6, 71). And if there were none of the Church but good men as long as they were good, then had St Peter been once no part of the Church after that Christ had appointed him for chief. But our Lord in this his mystical body of his Church, carried his members some sick, some whole, and all sickly. Nor they be not for every sin clean cast off from the body, but if they be for fear of infection cut off or else willingly do depart and separate himself as do these heretics, that either refuse the Church wilfully themself, or else for their obstinacy be put out. For till their stubborn hearts do show them incurable, that body beareth them yet about sick and naughty and key-cold as they be, to prove whether the warmness of grace going through this whole mystical body of Christ's Church might get yet and keep some life in them. But when the time shall come that this Church shall whole change her place and have heaven for her dwelling instead of earth, after the final judgment pronounced and given, when God shall with his spouse, this Church of Christ, enter into the pleasant wedding chamber to the bed of eternal rest, the shall all these mean and contemptible pieces scale clean off, and the whole body of Christ's holy Church remain pure, clean and glorious without stain, wrinkle or spot, which is—and for the while I believe will be, as long as she is here—as scabbed as ever was Job. And yet her loving spouse leaveth her not, but continually goeth about by many manner medicines, some bitter, some sweet, some easy, some grievous, some pleasant, some painful, to cure her. *(185)*

19. Now because that this world is, as I tell you, not our eternal dwelling, but our little while wandering, God would that we should in such wise use it as folk that are weary of it, and that we should in this vale of labour, toil, tears and misery, not look for rest and ease, game, pleasure, wealth and felicity. For they that so do fare like a fond fellow that going towards his own house where he should be wealthy, would for a tapster's pleasure become an ostler by the way and die in a stable and never come at home. And would God that those that drown themself in the desire of this world's wretched wealth, were not yet more fools than so! But alas! their folly as far passeth the foolishness of that other fond fellow as there is distance between the height of heaven and the very depth of hell. *(1154)*

20. The final fight is by invocation of help unto God both praying for himself and desiring other also to pray for him, both poor folk for his alms and other good folk of their charity, specially good priests in that holy sacred service of the Mass, and not only them, but also his own good angel and other holy saints such as his devotion specially stand unto. Or if he be learned, use then the Litany with the holy suffrages that follow, which is a prayer in the Church of marvellous old antiquity. *(1198)*

21. Master Lieutenant [of the Tower], I do not mislike my cheer, but whensoever I do, then thrust me out of your doors. *(38*)*

22. If we would well advise us upon this point and

remember the painful peril of death that we shall so soon come to, and that of all that we gather we shall carry nothing with us, it would cause us to consider that this covetous gathering and niggardous keeping, with all the delight that we take in the beholding of our substance, is in all our life but a very gay golden dream, in which we dream that we have great riches, and in the sleep of this life we be glad and proud thereof. But when death shall once waken us, our gay golden dream shall vanish and of all the treasure that we so merrily dreamed of, we shall not (as the holy prophet saith) find one penny left in our hands. Which if we forget not, but well and effectually remembered, we would in time cast covetousness out of our heads and leaving little business for our executors after our death, not fail to dispose and distribute our substance with our own hands. *(95)*

23. But let us that are no better than men of a mean sort, ever pray for such merciful amendment in other folk as our conscience sheweth us that we have need in ourself. *(1421)*

24. The cause of our salvation is not the belief in the promise nor the trust therein neither, or any proper nature of that belief in the promise, no more than the nature of our good works is able of itself for our salvation, but the ordinance of God, that it pleaseth him to save us for our obedience of his commandment, both in the belief and in the work. *(560)*

25. But now doth all good Christian people very well perceive by Christ's own promise in the very written gospel, that the Church of Christ is taught by his Holy Spirit, that these sacraments and ceremonies do please

God. And they perceive and see also that the holy saints which have used them before our day, be now long ago rewarded in heaven with God. And they perceive also that in the use thereof their minds risen and be lift up aloft in devotion to God. *(413)*

26. For surely the very best way were neither to read this book nor those of heretics, but rather the people unlearned to occupy themsel beside their other business in prayer, good meditation, and reading of such English books as most may nourish and increase devotion. Of which kind is Bonaventure of the life of Christ [*Speculam vitæ Christi*], Gerson of the following of Christ [*De Imitatione Christi*], and the devout contemplative book *Scala Perfectionis* [Hilton], with such other like, than in learning what may well be answered unto heretics. *(356)*

27. For I verily suppose that if there were a great king that had so tender love to a servant of his that he had, to help him out of danger, forsaken and left off all his worldly wealth and royalty and became poor and needy for his sake, that servant could hardly be found that were of such an unkind villain courage that if he himself came after to some substance, would not with better will lose it all again than shamefully to forsake such a master. And therefore, as I say, I do surely suppose that if we would well remember and inwardly consider the great goodness of our Saviour towards us, not yet being his poor sinful servants, but rather his adversaries and his enemies, and what wealth of this world that he willingly forsook for our sake, being indeed universal king thereof, and so having the power of his own hand to have used it if he had would, instead whereof, to make us rich in heaven, he lived here in

neediness and poverty all his life, and neither would have authority nor keep neither lands nor goods; the deep consideration and earnest advisement of this one point alone were able to make any kind Christian man or woman well content rather for his sake again to give up all that ever God hath lent them (and lent them hath he all that ever they have) than unkindly and unfaithfully to forsake him. And him they forsake if that for fear they forsake the confessing of his Christian faith. *(1234)*

28. And yet is faith alone good to be kept, yea and the very pieces and fragments of the faith also, for they be means by which a man may the more easily come to the remnant that he hath lost or lacketh. And they help with God's further help to keep a man from some sin though they keep him not from all. *(712)*

29. Many things know we that we seldom think on, and in the things of the soul, the knowledge without the remembrance little profiteth. What availeth to know that there is a God, which thou not only believest by faith but also knowest by reason, what availeth that thou knowest him, if thou think little of him? *(76)*

30. And if it be a thing detestable for any creature to rise in pride upon the respect and regard of person-age, beauty, strength, wit or learning or other such manner thing as by nature and grace are properly their own, how much more foolish abuse is there in that pride by which we worldly folk look up on height and solemn-ly set by ourself with deep disdain of other far better men, only for very vain worldly trifles that properly be not our own. *(1272)*

31. And now may you, methinketh, very plainly perceive that this whole earth is not only for all the whole kind of man a very plain prison indeed, but also that every man without exception, even those that are most at their liberty therein, and reckon themselves great lords and possessioners of very great pieces thereof, and thereby grow with wantonness so forgetful of their own state that they believe they stand in great wealth— do stand, for all that indeed, by the reason of their imprisonment in this large prison of the whole earth, in the selfsame condition that other do stand, which in the narrow prisons, which only be called prisons, and which only be reputed prisons in the opinion of the common people, stand in the fearful and in the most odious case, that is to wit, condemned already to death. *(1244)*

JUNE

1. *Good Lord, give me the grace so to spend my life, that when the day of my death shall come, though I feel pain in my body, I may feel comfort in soul, and with faithful hope of thy mercy, in due love towards thee and charity towards the world, I may, through thy grace, part hence into thy glory.* (1299)

2. How proud be men of gold and silver, no part of ourself but of the earth and of nature no better than is the poor copper and tin, nor to man's use so profitable as is the poor metal that maketh us the ploughshare and horseshoes and horsenails. *(1272)*

3. But now a Christian man that hath the light of faith, he cannot fail to think in this thing much farther. For he will think not only upon his bare coming hither and his bare going hence again, but also upon the dreadful judgement of God, and upon the fearful pains of hell, and the inestimable joys of heaven. But now to the intent he may think on such things the better, let him use often to resort to confession, and there open his heart, and by the mouth of some virtuous spiritual father have such things oft renewed in his remembrance. Let him also choose himself some secret solitary place in his own house, as far from noise and company as he conveniently can, and thither let him sometime secretly resort alone, imagining himself as one going out of the world, even straight into the giving up of his reckoning unto God of his sinful living. Then let him there before an altar, or some pitiful image of Christ's bitter passion (the beholding whereof may put

him in remembrance of the thing, and move him to devout compassion) kneel down or fall prostrate as at the feet of Almighty God, verily believing him to be there invisibly present as without any doubt he is. There let him open his heart to God and confess his faults such as he can call to mind, and pray God of forgiveness. Let him call to remembrance the benefits that God hath given him either in general among other men, or privately to himself, and give humble hearty thanks therefor. There let him declare unto God the temptations of the devil, the suggestions of the flesh, the occasions of the world, and of his worldly friends, much worse many times in drawing a man from God than are his most mortal enemies. Which thing our Saviour witnesseth himself where he saith, "The enemies of a man are they that are his familiars" (Matt. 10, 36). There let him lament bewail unto God his own frailty, negligence, and sloth in resisting and withstanding of temptations, his readiness and proneness to fall thereunto. There let him lamentably beseech God of his gracious aid and help, to strength his infirmity withal, both in keeping him from falling, and when he by his own fault misfortuneth to fall, then with the helping hand of his merciful grace to lift him up and set him on his feet in the state of his grace again, and let this man not doubt but that God heareth him and granted him gladly his boon. *(1201)*

4. If he have cause to fear, yet feareth he more than he needeth; for there is no devil so diligent to destroy him as God is to preserve him, nor no devil so near him to do him harm as God is to do him good; nor all the devils in hell so strong to invade and assault him as God is to defend him, if he distrust him not but faithfully put his trust in him. *(1197)*

5. Many men are there with whom God is not content, which abuse this great high goodness of his, whom neither fair treating, nor hard handling, can cause to remember their Maker; but in wealth they be wanton and forget God, and follow their lust, and when God with tribulation draweth them toward him, then grow they angry, and draw back all that ever they may, and rather run and seek help at any other hand than to go fetch it at his. Some for comfort seek to the flesh, some to the world, and some to the devil himself. Some man that in worldly prosperity is very dull, and hath deep stepped into many a sore sin, which sins, when he did them, he counted for part of his pleasure, God willing of his goodness to call the man to grace, casteth a remorse into his mind among after his first sleep, and maketh him lie a while and bethink him. *(1161)*

6. Now though a man without patience can have no reward for his pain, yet his pain is patiently taken for God's sake, and his will conformed to God's pleasure therein, God rewardeth the sufferer after the rate of his pain. *(1165)*

7. For other commandment had I never of his Grace [the King] in good faith, saving that this proviso his Highness added thereto that I should look first unto God and after God unto him, which word was also the first lesson that his Grace gave me what time I came first into his noble service and neither a more impartial commandment nor a more gracious lesson could there in my mind never King gave his counsellor or any his other servant. *(1443)*

8. For as God could, if it so pleased him, bring us all into the bliss of heaven without any good work at all,

so could he, if he list, bring us all thither without any faith at all. For he could bring us thither without any knowledge given us thereof, till we came thither and had it. So it appeareth clearly that the cause of salvation standeth all in the obedience of God's commandment, whereby he biddeth us, and by his bidding bindeth us, to continue our understanding into the obedience of faith and believe his promises. *(560)*

9. For better is yet of truth a conscience a little too strait than a little too large. *(1183)*

10. For some man that falleth to theft, sometime remembereth yet his baptism, and being by the devil enticed to kill the man, maketh a cross upon his breast and prayeth Christ keep him from it and in adultery likewise. And God in that good mind assisteth the man by grace and worketh with his will in keeping him therefrom, as he gave him good thoughts and offered him his grace if he would have taken hold thereof to keep him from the other too. *(712)*

11. What meaneth our Lord by his parable of the ten virgins, five fools and five wise abiding and looking for the spouse that should come to the marriage? Meant he not plainly the whole company present here in this world, of which though all bring the lamps of faith, yet some forsooth lack the oil of good works, for which their faith alone lacking the light of grace shall find the gate of glory shut against them, when the spouse with the wise virgins shall be gone in? *(824)*

12. So help me God and none otherwise, but as I verily think that many a man buyeth hell with so much pain that he might have heaven with less than one half. *(1203)*

13. And verily thought it be, as indeed it is, easy enough for any man to say the word that he is here but a pilgrim, yet it is hard for many a man to let it fall feelingly and sink down deep into his breast, which against that world slightly spoken once in a year, useth to rejoice and boast many times a day by the space peradventure of many years together, what goodly places in this world he hath of his own, in every which continually he calleth himself at home. And that such folk reckon themselves not for pilgrims here, they feel full well at such time as our Lord calleth them hence. For then find they themselves much more loath to part from this world than pilgrims to go from their inn. *(1313)*

14. "What the good year, Master More," quoth Mistress Alice, "I marvel that you, that have been always hitherto taken for so wise a man, will now so play the fool to lie here in this close, filthy prison, and be content thus to be shut up among mice and rats, when you might be abroad at your liberty, and with the favour and good will both of the King and his Council, if you would but do as all the Bishops and best learned of this Realm have done. And seeing you have at Chelsea a right fair house, your library, your books, your gallery your orchard and all other necessities so handsome about you, where you might have the company of me your wife, your children and household be merry, I muse what a God's name you mean here still thus fondly to tarry."

After he had a while quietly heard her, with a cheerful countenance he said unto her, "I pray thee, good Mistress Alice, tell me one thing."

"What is that?" quoth she.

"Is not this house", quoth he, "as nigh heaven as my own?"

To whom she, after her accustomed homely fashion, not liking such talk, answered, "Tilly-vally, tilly-vally!"

"How say you, Mistress Alice," quoth he, "is it not so?"

"Bone deus, bone deus, man, will this gear never be left?" quoth she.

"Well then, Mistress Alice, if it be so," quoth he, "it is very well. For I see no great cause why I should much joy either of my gay house or of anything belonging thereunto, when, if I should but seven years lie buried under the ground, and then arise and come thither again, I should not fail to find some therein that would bid me get out of doors, and tell me it were none of mine. What cause have I then to like such a house as would so soon forget his master?" *(40*)*

15. I never saw a fool yet but thought himself other than wise. For as it is one spark of soberness left in a drunken head when he perceiveth himself drunk and getteth him fair to bed, so if a fool perceive himself a fool, that point is no folly but a little spark of wit. *(1251)*

16. But now having the full faith of this point fastly grounded in our heart, that the thing which we receive is the very blessed body of Christ, I trust there shall not greatly need any great information farther to teach us, or any great exhortation farther to stir and excite us, with all humble manner and reverent behaviour to receive him. For if we will consider, if there were a great worldly prince which for special favour that he bare us would come visit us in our own house, what a business we would then make, and what a work it would be for us, to see that our house were trimmed up in every point, to the best of our possible power, and

everything so provided and ordered that he should by
his honourable receiving perceive what affection we
bear him, and in what high estimation we have him;
we should soon by the comparing of that worldly
prince and this heavenly prince together (between
which twain is far less comparison than is between a
man and a mouse) inform and teach ourself with how
lowly mind, how tender loving heart, how reverent
humble manner we should endeavour ourself to receive
this glorious heavenly king, the king of kings, Almighty
God himself, that so lovingly doth vouchsafe to enter,
not only into our house (to which the noble Centurion
acknowledged himself unworthy) but his precious body
into our vile wretched carcase, and his Holy Spirit
into our poor simple soul. What diligence can here
suffice us? What solicitude can we think here enough
against the coming of this almighty king, coming for so
special gracious favour, not to put us to cost, not to
spend of ours, but to enrich us of his, and that after
so manifold deadly displeasures done him so unkindly
by us, against so many of his incomparable benefits
before done unto us. How would we now labour and
foresee that the house of our soul (which God were
coming to rest in) should neither have any poisoned
spider or cobweb or deadly sin hanging in the roof, nor
so much as a straw or a feather of any light lewd thought
that we might spy on the floor, but we would sweep it
away. *(1267)*

17. *Give me, good Lord, a full faith, a firm hope, and a*
fervent charity, a love to the good Lord incomparable
above the love to myself, and that I love nothing to thy
displeasure, but everything in an order to thee. Give me,
good Lord, a longing to be with thee, not for the avoiding of
the calamities of this wretched world, nor so much for the

*avoiding the pains of purgatory, nor of the pains of hell
neither, nor so much for the attaining of the joys of heaven,
in respect of mine own commodity, as even for a very love
to thee. And bear me, good Lord, thy love and favour,
which thing my love to thee-ward (were it never so great)
could not but of thy great goodness deserve. (1417)*

18. Now touching the evil petitions; though they
that ask them were, as I trust they be not, a great
people, they be not yet so many that ask evil petitions of
saints as there be that ask the same of God himself.
For whatsoever they will ask of any good saint they
will ask of God also. And commonly in the wild Irish,
and some in Wales too, as men say, when they go
forth in robbing, they bless them and pray God send
them good speed that they may meet with a good purse
and do harm and take none. Shall we therefore find a
fault with every man's prayer because thieves pray for
speed in robbery? This hath, as I say, no reason,
although they were a great people and abused a good
thing. And whereas the worst that ye assign in our
matter is that, as ye say, the people do idolatry in that
ye say they take the images for saints themselves or the
rood for Christ himself, which as I said I think none
doth, for some rood hath no crucifix thereon, and they
believe not that the cross which they see was ever at
Jerusalem, nor that it was the holy cross itself; and much
less think they then that the image that hangeth thereon
is the body of Christ himself. And although some were
so mad so to think, yet were it not, as ye call it, the
people. For a few doting dames make not the people.
And over this, if it were, as ye would have it seem, an
whole people indeed, yet were it not a good thing to be
put away for the misuse of bad folk. *(199)*

19. Let them that are in the troublous fear of their
own scrupulous conscience, submit the rule of their
own conscience to the counsel of some other good man,
which, after the variety and the nature of scruples, may
temper his advice. Yea, although a man be very learned
himself, yet let him in this case learn the custom used
by physicians. For be one of them never so cunning,
yet in his own disease and sickness he never useth to
trust all to himself, but sendeth for such of his fellows
as he knoweth fit, and putteth himself in their hands
for many considerations, whereof they assign the
causes. And one of the causes is fear, whereof upon
some tokens he may conceive in his own passion a great
deal more than needeth. *(1186)*

20. He feareth also where he needeth not. For where
he dreadeth that he were out of God's favour because
such horrible thoughts fall into his mind, he must
understand that while they fall in his mind against his
will, they be therefore not imputed unto him. He is
finally sad of that he may be glad. For since he taketh
such thoughts displeasantly and striveth and fighteth
against them, he hath thereby a token that he is in
God's favour, and that God assisteth him and helpeth
him, and may make himself sure that so will God
never cease to do, but if himself fail and fall from him
first. And over that, this conflict that he hath against
his temptation shall, if he will not fall where he needeth
not, be an occasion of his merit and a right great reward
in heaven. *(1197)*

21. Master Cromwell, you are now entered upon the
service of a most noble, wise and liberal Prince. If you
will you will follow my poor advice, you shall, in your
counsel giving unto his Grace, ever tell him what he

ought to do, but never what he is able to do. So shall you shew yourself a true faithful servant and a right worthy councillor. For if a lion knew his own strength, hard were it for any man to rule him. *(28*)*

22. If thou knewest very certainly that after all thy goods gathered together, thou shouldst be suddenly robbed of all together, thou wouldst, I believe, have little joy to labour and toil for so much, but rather as thou shouldst happen to get it, so wouldst thou wisely bestow it there as need were thou mightest have thank therefor, and on them specially that were likely to help thee with theirs when thine were all gone. But it is so that thou art of nothing so sure as that death shall bereave thee of all that thou heapest, and leave thee scant a sheet. Which thing, if we did as well remember as we well know, we should not fail to labour less for that we shall so lose, and would put into poor men's purses our money to keep, that death, the cruel thief, should not find it about us, but they should relieve us therewith when the remnant were bereft us. *(95)*

23. Many which right surely believe the mercy of God, do not yet love God in such wise as is required unto salvation, that is in preferring his pleasure before their own and to forbear sin for the love of his law and for the regard of his goodness to fulfil his commandments. But we find it many times far contrary that the overgreat regard of his mercy turneth trust into presumption and maketh men the more bold to sin, so forsooth that neither love of God, nor desire of heaven, nor dread of hell, is able to pull them back. *(584)*

24. In devising whereupon, albeit, mine own good daughter, that I found myself, I cry God mercy, very

sensual and my flesh much more shrinking from pain
and from death than me thought it the part of a faithful
Christian man, in such a case as my conscience gave me,
that in the saving of my body should stand the loss of
my soul; yet I thank our Lord, that in that conflict, the
Spirit had in conclusion the mastery, and reason with
help of faith finally concluded that for to be put to
death wrongfully for doing well (as I am very sure I do,
in refusing to swear against mine own conscience,
being such as I am not upon peril of my soul bounden
to change whether my death should come without law,
or by colour of a law) it is a case in which a man may
lose his head and yet have none harm, but instead of
harm inestimable good at the hand of God. *(1446)*

25. It is good alway to be doing some good out of
hand while we think thereon; grace shall the better
stand with us and increase also to go the farther in the
other after. *(1207)*

26. Many a man that hath a great wit and a great
reason too, and much learning joined unto them both,
doth yet more foolishly and more unreasonably than
doth some other whose wit and reason is very far under
his, and as for learning hath utterly none at all. And
whereof cometh this? But in that the one with no
learning and no great wit hath great good will to work
with God's grace and do well, and the other with much
wit and learning, lacketh the will to work well after
his reason, and therefore letteth grace go by and wilfully
followeth affection. *(585)*

27. I said that I was very sure that mine own conscience so informed as it is by such diligence as I have so
long taken therein may stand with mine own salvation.

I meddle not with the conscience of them that think otherwise, every man *suo domino stat et cadit:* before his own master stands or falls. I am no man's judge. It was also said unto me that if I had as gladly be out of the world as in it, as I had there said, why did I not speak even out plain against the statute [of Succession]. It appeared well I was not content to die though I said so. Whereunto I answered, as the truth is that I have not been a man of such holy living as I might be bold to offer myself to death, lest God for my presumption might suffer me to fall, and therefore I put not myself forward but draw back. Howbeit if God draw me to it himself, then trust I in his great mercy that he shall not fail to give me grace and strength. *(1453)*

28. That you fear your own frailty, Marget, nothing misliketh me. God give us both twain the grace to despair of our own self and whole to depend and hang upon the hope and strength of God. *(1449)*

29. And verily, my dear daughter, in this is my great comfort, that albeit I am of nature so shrinking from pain that I am almost afeard of a fillip, yet in all the agonies that I have had, whereof before my coming hither [the Tower], as I have showed you ere this, I have had neither small nor few, with heavy fearful heart, forecasting all such perils and painful deaths as by any manner of possibility might after fall unto me, and in such thought lain long restless and waking while my wife had thought I had slept, yet in any such fear and heavy pensiveness, I thank the mighty mercy of God, I never in my mind intended to consent, that I would for the enduring of the uttermost, do any such thing as I should in mine own conscience (for with other men's I am not a man meet to take upon me to meddle) think

to be to myself such as should damnably cast me in the displeasure of God. And this is the least point that any man may with his salvation come to, as far as I can see, and is bounden if he see peril to examine his conscience surely by learning and by good counsel and be sure that his conscience be such as it may stand with his salvation, or else reform it. And if the matter be such, as both the parties may stand with salvation, then on whither side his conscience fall, he is safe enough before God. But that mine own may stand with my own salvation, thereof I thank our Lord I am very sure. I beseech our Lord bring all parties to his bliss. *(1449)*

30. But since God hath shewed you plainly by reason that he hath given his Church in all things knowledge of the truth, if ye will take the sure way and put yourself out of all perplexity in the point itself, and the Scriptures that touch it, ye shall take for the truth that way that the Church teacheth you therein howsoever that matter seem beside unto yourself or any man else. *(172)*

JULY

1. Therefore am I not bound to conform my conscience to the Council of one Realm against the General Council of Christendom. *(46*)*

2. More have I not to say, my lords, but that like the Blessed Apostle St Paul, as we read in the Acts of the Apostles, was present, and consented to the death of St Stephen and kept their clothes that stoned him to death, and yet be they now both twain Holy Saints in heaven, and shall continue there friends for ever, so I verily trust and shall therefore right heartily pray, that though your lordships have now here in earth been judges to my condemnation, we may hereafter in heaven merrily all meet together, to our everlasting salvation. *(47*)*

3. I have lived, methinks, a long life and now neither I look nor I long to live much longer. I have since I came in the Tower looked once or twice to have given up my spirit ere this and in good faith mine heart grew the lighter with hope thereof. Yet forget I not that I have a long reckoning and a great to give account of, but I put my trust in God and in the merits of his bitter passion, and I beseech him give me and keep me the mind to long to be out of this world and to be with him. For I can never but trust that who so long to be with him shall be welcome to him and on the other side my mind giveth me verily that any that ever shall come to him shall full heartily wish to be with him or ever he shall come at him. *(1443)*

4. And yet I know well for all this mine frailty, and

that St Peter which feared it much less than I, fell in such fear soon after, that at the word of a simple girl he forsook and forswore Our Saviour. And therefore am I not, Meg, so mad as to warrant myself to stand. But I shall pray, and I pray thee, mine own good daughter, to pray with me, that it may please God that hath given me this mind, to give me the grace to keep it. *(1447)*

5. I cumber you good Margaret much, but I would be sorry if it should be any longer than tomorrow for it is St Thomas even and the octave of St Peter and therefore tomorrow long I to go to God, it were a day very meet and convenient for me. Farewell, my dear child, and pray for me, and I shall for you and all your friends that we may merrily meet in heaven. *(1457)*

6. And so was he by Master Lieutenant brought out of the Tower and from thence led towards the place of execution. Where, going up the scaffold, which was so weak that it was ready to fall, he said merrily to Master Lieutenant, "I pray you, Master Lieutenant, see me safe up, and for my coming down let me shift for myself." *(50*)*

HE THEN EARNESTLY ENTREATED THEM TO PRAY FOR THE KING SO THAT GOD WOULD GIVE HIM GOOD COUNSEL, AND SOLEMNLY DECLARED THAT HE DIED THE KING'S GOOD SERVANT BUT GOD'S FIRST.

7. The martyrs in their agony made no long prayers aloud, but one inch of such a pray so prayed in that pain was worth a whole ell and more even of their own prayers prayed at some other time. *(1164)*

8. And surely I doubt it a little in my mind but that if a man had in his heart so deep a desire and love, longing to be with God in heaven, to have the fruition of his glorious face, as had those holy men that were martyrs in old time, he would no more shrink from the pain that he must pass between that at that time those old holy martyrs did. *(1218)*

9. But first I think it better to bestow some time upon another thing, and, leaving for a while both defence of my own faults and finding of other men's in writing, think better to bestow some time about the mending of mine own in living, which is a thing now for many men more necessary than is writing. For of new book makers there are now more than enough. Wherefore that all such as will write may have the grace to write well, or at the least wise none other purpose than to mean well, and as well writers as other to amend our own faults and live well, I beseech Almighty God to grant us and that all folk spiritual and temporal in this world living, and all good Christian souls departed hence and yet not out of pain, may for grace every part pray for other and all the blessed saints in heaven, both here for grace and there for glory, pray to God for us all. *(928)*

10. Tribulation gains merit in patience, and in the obedient conforming of the man's will unto God, and in thanks given to God for his visitation. *(1166)*

11. It was not for nought ordained by the apostles that in the dreadful mysteries of the Mass, should commemoration be made for them that be dead. For the apostles knew that thereby cometh to the souls great advantage and profit. For when all the people standeth together, holding up their hands, and the priest ful-

filleth his observance, and that dreadful sacrifice set forth, how can it be but that then praying for the souls, we shall obtain? *(518)*

12. Then shall we consider tribulation as a gracious gift of God, a gift that he specially gave his special friends, the thing that in Scripture is highly commended and praised, a thing whereof the contrary long continued is perilous, a thing which, but if God send it, men have need by penance to put upon themself and seek it, a thing that helpeth to purge our sins passed, a thing that preserveth us from sins that else would come, a thing that causeth us to set less by the world, a thing that exciteth us to draw more toward God, a thing that much deminisheth our pains in purgatory, a thing that much increaseth our final reward in heaven, the thing by which Our Saviour entered his own kingdom, the thing with which all his apostles followed him thither, the thing which Our Saviour exhorteth all men to, the thing without which, he saith, we be not his disciples, the thing without which no man can get to heaven. *(1168)*

13. Would God that all the prelates, and all curates, and all preachers, yea and fathers and mothers and all masters of households too, could here of Our Saviour take example for to give good example. There are many that can be well content to be preaching, some to show their cunning and some to show their authority. But would God they would use the fashion that Our Saviour used, that is to wit, the things that they bid other men do, do it first themself. *(1319)*

14. How proud is many a man over his neighbour because the wool of his gown is finer, and yet as fine as it is, a poor sheep wore it on her back before it came

upon his, and all the while she wore it, were her wool never so fine, yet was she, verily, but a sheep. And why should he be now better than she by that wool, that though it be his, is yet not so verily his, as it was verily hers? *(1272)*

15. If we see cockle in the Church, yet should neither our faith nor our charity be forsaken or hindred thereby, so that because we see cockle in the Church, we would ourself therefore go from the Church. Let us no more but labour that we may be corn ourself, that when the corn shall be laid up in the garners of God, we may of our works and labour receive the fruit. *(826)*

16. But forasmuch, good Christian reader, as we neither can attain this great point of faith (that the thing which we receive is the very blessed body of Christ) nor any other virtue but by the special grace of God, of whose high goodness every good thing cometh—for as St James saith: "Every good gift and every perfect gift is from above, descending from the father of lights" *(1-17)* —let us therefore pray for his gracious help in the attaining of his faith, and for his help in the cleaning of our soul against his coming, that he may make us worthy to receive him worthily. And ever let us of our own part fear our unworthiness, and on his part trust boldly upon his goodness, if we are not slow to work with him for our part. For if we willingly upon the trust and comfort of his goodness leave our own endeavour undone, then is our hope no hope, but a very foul presumption. Then when we come unto his holy board, into the presence of his blessed body, let us consider his high glorious majesty which his high goodness there hideth from us, and the proper form of his holy flesh covereth under the form of bread, both to keep us from

abashment such as we could not peradventure abide, if we (such as we yet be) should see and receive him in his own form such as he is, and also for the increase of the merit of our faith in the obedient belief of that thing at his commandment, whereof our eyes and our reason seem to show us the contrary. And yet forasmuch as although we believe it, yet is there, in many of us that believe, very faint and far from the point of such vigour and strength as would God it had, let us say unto him with the father that had the dumb son, "I believe, Lord, but help thou my lack of belief" (Mark 9, 23), and with his blessed apostles, "Lord, increase faith in us" (Luke 17, 5). Let is also with the poor publican, in knowledge of our own unworthiness, say with all meekness of heart, "Lord God, be merciful to me, sinner that I am" (Luke 18, 13). And with the Centurion, "Lord, I am not worthy that thou shouldst come into my house" (Matt. 8, 8). And yet with all this remembrance of our own unworthiness and therefore the great reverence, fear and dread for our own part, let us not forget on the other side to consider his inestimable goodness, which disdaineth not, for all our unworthiness, to come unto us and to be received of us. But likewise as at the sight and receiving of this excellent memorial of his death (for in the remembrance thereof doth he thus consecrate and give his own blessed flesh and blood unto us) we must with tender compassion, remember and call to mind the bitter pains of his most pitiful passion. And yet therewithal rejoice and be glad in the consideration of his incomparable kindness, which in his so suffering for us, to our inestimable benefit he showed and declared towards us. So must we be both sore afeard of our unworthiness, and yet therewith be right glad and in great hope at the consideration of his unmeasurable goodness. *(1267)*

17. *And pardon me, good Lord, that I am so bold as to ask so high petitions, being so vile a sinful wretch, and so unworthy to attain the lowest. But yet, good Lord, such they be, as I am bounden to wish and should be nearer the effectual desire of them, if my manifold sins were not the let. From which, O glorious Trinity, vouchsafe of thy goodness to wash me, with that blessed blood that issued out of thy tender body, O sweet Saviour Christ, in the divers torments of thy most bitter passion. (1417)*

18. And therefore let us never make reckoning of long life; keep it while we may because God hath so commanded. But if God give the occasion that with his good will we may go, let us be glad thereof and long to go to him. And then shall hope of heaven comfort our heaviness, and out of our transitory tribulation shall we go to everlasting glory. *(1169)*

19. Our affection toward heavenly joys groweth wonderful cold. If dread of hell were as far gone, very few would fear God; but that yet a little sticketh in our stomachs. Mark me, at the sermon, and commonly towards the end, somewhat the preacher speaketh of hell and heaven. Now while he preacheth the pains of hell, still they stand and yet give him the hearing, but as soon as he cometh to the joys of heaven, they be drawing back and one and all fall away. *(1171)*

20. Out of the case of such extreme needs well perceived and known unto myself, I am not bounden to give every beggar that will ask, nor to believe every impostor that I meet in the street that will say himself that he is very sick, nor to reckon all the poor folk committed by God only so to my charge alone, that none other man should give them nothing of his, till

I have first given out all mine; nor am I bounden neither to have so evil an opinion of all other folk save myself, as to think that but if I help the poor folk shall all fail at once, for God hath left in all this quarter no more good folk now but me. I may think better by my neighbours, and worse by myself than so, and yet come to heaven by God's grace well enough. *(1209)*

21. A merry tale with a friend refresheth a man much and without any harm lighteth his mind and amendeth his courage and his stomach. *(1171)*

22. But yet though God, I doubt not, be so merciful unto them that at any time in their life turn and ask his mercy and trust therein, though it be at the last end of a man's life, and hireth him as well for heaven that cometh to work in his vineyard toward night, at such time as workmen leave work and go home (being then in will to work if the time would serve) as he hireth him that cometh in the morning; yet may there no man upon the trust of this parable be bold all his life to lie still in sin. For let him remember that into God's vineyard there goeth no man but he that is called thither. Now, he that in hope to be called toward night, will sleep out the morning and drink out the day, is full likely to pass at night unspoken to, and then shall he go supperless to bed. *(1174)*

23. I counsel him that cannot be sad for his sin, to be sorry at the least that he cannot be sorry. *(1176)*

24. And therefore can we not doubt, if we follow God, and with faithful hope come run unto him, but that he shall in all matter of temptation take us near unto him, and set us even under his wing, and then are we safe

if we will tarry there. For against our will can there no power pull us thence nor hurt our souls there. *(1179)*

25. For since Our Lord hath now done so much for us, as in such abundance of his coming, to give out his grace unto us, that we may with help thereof being so plenteous, with much less difficulty much more resist the flesh, and much more follow the spirit, and keep the spirit with us, and for the spirit inhabiting within us merit much more glory, first in soul, and after in body, which the Father of Our Saviour that raiseth his, that for the same spirit inhabiting in us, raise and resuscitate to bliss, therefore are we doctors, saith St Paul, and it is our bounden duty to follow not the flesh whom we may now by the plenteous grace of God so well and easily resist, and whose affections if we follow we shall die, but the Spirit of God, and by that Spirit to mortify the deeds and works of the flesh, which if we do we shall live. *(700)*

26. Lo, St Paul, though God withdrew not his hand and help from him, had yet such a plague of temptation (2 Cor. xii, 7) put upon him, that he grew weary thereof and very sore afeard. And wherefore was it laid to his charge, lest he should have thought his virtue to come of himself? Nay, lest he might through the great revelations that he had had, fall into pride and presumption. *(590)*

27. To some that are good men God sendeth wealth here also, and they give him great thank for his gift and he rewardeth them for that thank too. To some good folk he sendeth sorrow and they thank him thereof too. If God should give the goods of this world only to evil folk, then would men believe that God were not the

Lord thereof. If God would give the goods only to good men, then would folk take occasion to serve him but for them. *(1157)*

28. In the fervent heat of every temptation, God giveth the faithful man that hopeth in him the shadow of his holy shoulders, which are broad and large, sufficient to cool and refresh the man in that heat, and in every tribulation he putteth his shoulders for a defence between. And then what weapon of the devil may give us any deadly wound while that impenetrable shield of the shoulder of God standeth alway between? *(1179)*

29. He first without writing revealed those heavenly mysteries by his blessed mouth through the ears of his apostles and disciples into their holy hearts; or rather, as it seemeth, it was inwardly infused into St Peter, his heart, by the secret inspiration of God without either writing or any outward word. For which cause, when he had upon Christ's question demanding "Of whom say you that I am?", answered and said, "Thou art Christ the son of the living God which art come into this world." Our Saviour said again unto him, "Thou art blessed, Simon the son of Jona, for neither flesh nor blood hath revealed and shewed this to thee, but my Father that is in heaven" (Matt. 16, 13-17). And thus it appeareth that the faith came in to St Peter, his heart, as to the prince of the apostles, without hearing, by secret inspiration, and into the remnant by his confession and Christ's holy mouth. And by them in like manner—first without writing, by only words and preaching, so was it spread abroad in the world that his faith was by the mouths of his holy messengers put into men's ears, and by his holy hand written in men's hearts, or ever any word thereof almost was written in

the book. And so was it convenient for the law of life rather to be written in the lively minds of men than in the dead skins of beasts. And I nothing doubt but all had it so been that never gospel had been written, yet should the substance of this faith never have fallen out of Christian folk's hearts, but the same spirit that planted it, the same should have watered it, the same should have kept it, the same should have increased it. But so hath it liked our Lord, after his high wisdom, to provide that some of his disciples have written many things of his holy life, doctrine and faith, and yet far from all which, as St John saith, the world could not have comprehended. *(158)*

30. This pusillanimity bringeth forth by the night's fear a very timorous daughter, a foolish wretched girl and ever puling, that is called scrupulosity or a scrupulous conscience. This girl is a fairly good maid-servant in a house, never idle, but ever occupied and busy. But albeit she hath a very gentle mistress that loveth her well, and is well content with that she doth, or if it be not all well, as all cannot always be well, content to pardon her as she doth other of her fellows and so letteth her know that she will; yet can this peevish girl never cease whining and puling for fear lest her mistress be alway angry with her and that she shall sharply be scolded. Were her mistress, think you, like to be content with this condition? Nay, surely. I knew such one myself, whose mistress was a very wise woman, and, which thing is in women rare, very mild and also meek, and liked very well such service as she did her in the house, but this continual discomfortable fashion of hers she so much misliked that she would sometime say, "Eh, what aileth this girl? The elvish urchin thinketh I were a devil, I believe. Surely if she did me ten

times better service than she doth, yet with this fantastical fear of hers, I would be loath to have her in my house." Thus fareth, lo! the scrupulous person, which frameth himself many times double the fear that he hath cause, and many times a great fear where there is no cause at all, and of that that is indeed no sin, maketh a venial, and that that is venial, imagineth to be deadly, and yet, for all that, falleth in them, being namely of their nature such as no man long liveth without. And then he feareth that he be never full confessed, nor never full contrite, and then that his sins be never full forgiven him, and then he confesseth, and confesseth again, and cumbereth himself and his confessor both. With this night's fear the devil sore troubleth the mind of many a right good man, and that doth he, to bring him to some great inconvenience, for he will, if he can, drive him so much to the fearful minding of God's rigorous justice, that he will keep him from the comfortable remembrance of God's great mighty mercy, and so make him do all his good works wearily, and without consolation or quickness. *(1182)*

31. For likewise as some man going over an high bridge becomes so afeard through his own fantasy that he falleth down indeed, which were else able enough to pass over without any danger; and as some man shall upon such a bridge, if folk call upon him, "You fall, you fall," fall with the fantasy that he taketh thereof, which bridge, if folk looked merrily upon him and said, there is no danger therein, he would pass over well enough, and would not hesitate to run thereon if it were but a foot from the ground; thus fareth it is this temptation. The devil findeth the man of his own fantasy afeard, and then crieth he in the ear of his heart, "Thou fallest, thou fallest," and maketh the fond man afraid that he should

at every foot fall indeed. And the devil so wearieth him with that continual fear, if he give the ear of his heart unto him, that at the last he withdraweth his mind from due remembrance of God and then driveth him to that deadly mischief indeed. Some folk have been clearly rid of such pestilent fantasies with the very full contempt thereof, making a cross upon their hearts and bidding the devil avaunt, and so sometime laugh him to scorn too, and then turn mind unto some other matter. *(1197)*

AUGUST

1. *My sweet Saviour Christ, whom thine own wicked disciple, entangled with the devil through vile wretched covetousness betrayed, inspire, I beseech thee, the marvel of thy majesty with the love of thy goodness, so deep into mine heart, that in respect of the least point of thy pleasure my mind may set always this whole wretched world at nought. (1305)*

2. Of saying service, this is much like as at Beverley, late, when much of the people being at a bear-baiting, the church fell suddenly down at evensong time and overwhelmed some that then were in it. A good fellow that after heard the tale told, "Lo," quod he, "now may you see what it is is to at evensong when you should be at the bear-baiting." Howbeit the hurt was not there in being at evensong, but in that the church was falsely wrought. So was in him, or any man else, none harm, but good in saying of divine service; but the occasion of harm is in the superstitious fashion that their own folly joineth thereunto—as some think they say it not but if they say every psalm twice. *(208)*

3. Now this know I very well that those that are walking about in this busy maze take not their business for any tribulation, and yet are there many of them wearied as sore, and as sore hurt and pained therein, their pleasures being so short, so little and so few, and their displeasures and their griefs so great, so continual and so many, that it maketh me think upon a good worshipful man, which when he divers times beheld his wife, what pain she took in straight binding up her hair

to make her a fair large forehead, and with strait bracing in her body to make her middle small, both twain to her great pain for the pride of a little foolish praise; he said unto her, "Forsooth, madam, if God give you not hell, he shall do you great wrong; for it must needs be your own of very right, for you buy it very dear, and take very great pain therefor." *(1205)*

4. Now tell me, then, if thou were going out of an house, whether art thou going out only when thy foot is on the uttermost inch of the threshold, thy body half out of the door, or else when thou beginnest to set the first foot forward to go out, in what place of the house soever ye stand when ye hurry forward? I would say that ye be going out of the house from the first foot ye set forward to go forth. No man will think other, as I suppose, but all is one reason in going hence and coming hither. Now if one were coming hither to this town, he were not only coming hither while he was entering in at the gate, but all the way also from whence he came hitherward. Nor, in likewise, in going hence from this town: a man is not only going from this town while he hath his body in the gate going outward, but also while he setteth foot out of his host's house to go forward. And therefore if a man met him by the way, far yet within the town, and asked him whither he were going, he should truly answer that he were going out of the town, all were the town so long that he had ten miles to go ere he came to the gate. And surely methinketh that in likewise a man is not only dying, that is to say going in his way out of this life, while he lieth drawing on, but also all the while that he is going towards his end, which is by all the whole time of his life, since the first moment till the last finished, that is to say, since the first moment in which he began to live, until the last

moment of his life, or rather the first in which he is fully dead. Now if this be thus, as meseemeth that reason proveth, a man is always dying from afore his birth, and every hour of our age, as it passeth by, cutteth his own length out of our life and maketh it shorter by so much, and our death so much the nearer. Which measuring of time and diminishing of life, with approaching towards death, is nothing else but from our beginning to our ending, one continual dying; so that wake we, sleep we, eat we, drink we, mourn we, sing we, in what wise soever live we, all the same while die we. So that we never ought to look towards death as a thing far off, considering that although he made no haste towards us, yet we never cease ourselves to make haste towards him. *(81)*

5. When I was first of the King's Council and after his Under-Treasurer and in the time while I was Chancellor of his Duchy of Lancaster, and when I was Chancellor of this realm, it was very well known what manner of favour I bare towards the clergy and that as I loved and honoured the good, so was not remiss nor slack in providing for the correction of those that were nought, vexatious to good people, and slanderous of their own order. Which sort of priests and religious running out of religion and falling to theft and murder, had at my hand so little favour that there was no man that any meddling had with them into whose hands they were more loath to come. *(867)*

6. Whosoever will mark the devil and his temptations shall find him therein much like to an ape. For like as an ape, not well looked unto, will be busy and bold to do mischievous turns, and contrariwise, being spied, will suddenly leap back and adventure no farther, so the

devil, finding a man idle, slothful and without resistance ready to receive his temptations, groweth so hardy that he will not fail still to continue with him, until to his purpose he have throughly brought him. But on the other side, if he see a man with diligence persevere to prevent and withstand his temptations, he groweth so weary that in conclusion he utterly forsaketh him. For as the devil of disposition is a spirit of so high a pride that he cannot abide to be mocked, so is he of nature so envious that he feareth any more to assault him, lest he should thereby not only catch a foul fall himself, but also minister to the man more matter of merit. *(15*)*

7. In believing the Church, we put not our trust in the men whom we believe, but we put our trust in God, for whom and by whom we believe the men. *(703)*

8. Covetousness is a very prisoner for he cannot get away. Pride will away with shame, envy with his enemy's misery, wrath with fair entreating, sloth with hunger and pain, lechery with sickness, gluttony with the belly too full, but covetousness can nothing get away. For the more full, the more greedy, and the older the more niggard, and the richer the more needy. *(1297)*

9. Unlearned men are not able, nor every learned man neither, surely to discern and judge the true sense of the Scripture, in a great thing grown in debate and controversy, where plain texts of Scripture seem to speak for both sides. And therefore it must needs be that there is by God provided and left some such surety as may bring us out of all such perplexity. And that is, as I have said, his Holy Spirit sent and left perpetually with his Church to lead it so by his own promise ever into all necessary truth. *(527)*

10. The most part I suppose that of the Christian people shall be damned, the cause of their damnation shall be that whereas they believe right and love God also, so far forth as he will let them live as they please and make merry, and bind them to nothing that they have no wish to do, love him not yet so sufficiently, as for the love they bear him, they will rather forbear the pleasures of their life, and also rather die than deadly to displease him by the doing of any such thing as he will rather that they should die than do it. *(606)*

11. But as men may call him a fool that beareth himself proud because he jetteth about in a borrowed gown, so may we be well called very fools all, if we bear us proud of anything that we have here. For nothing have we here of our own, not so much as our own bodies, but here borrowed it all of God, and yield it we must again, and send our foolish soul out naked no man can tell how soon. *(1272)*

12. If to the historical faith gotten by man, withal other good circumstances that man by possibility may put into it, God doth ever add and instil the feeling faith himself, supplying by the congruence of his own goodness the feebleness and lack of power upon the man's part toward attaining of his own salvation, being the great high gift of God so far above the proportion of man's natural state. *(730)*

13. He that biddeth other folk do well and giveth evil example with the contrary deed himself, fareth even like a foolish weaver that would weave a part with the one hand and unweave as fast with the other. *(1319)*

14. As for such venial sins as folk of fraility so com-

monly do fall in, that no man is almost any time without
them (though the profit would be more if men did think
they were mortal, so that the dread thereof could make
men utterly forbear them) yet, since it will not be that
men will utterly forbear them, the knowledge of the
truth is necessary for them, lest every time that they do
such a sin indeed, believing that it were mortal, the
doing of the deed, with the conscience of a mortal sin,
might make it mortal indeed. *(964)*

15. For it is almost a common thing among men so to
speak sometime as though they could amend the works
of God. And few men there be, I am sure, but they think
that if they had been of God's council in the making of
the world, though they dare not be so bold to say that
they could have made it better, yet, if they might have
ruled it, he should have made many things of another
fashion. And for all that, if he would yet call us to
council, and change nothing till we were upon everything
all agreed, the world were well likely till doomsday to go
forth on as it goeth already, saving that I doubt whether
we would agree to be winged. *(156)*

16. St Elizabeth at the visitation and salutation of Our
Blessed Lady, having by revelation the sure inward
knowledge that Our Lady was conceived of Our Lord,
albeit that she was herself such as else for the diversity
between their ages she well might and would have
thought it but convenient and meetly that her young
cousin should come visit her, yet now because she was
mother to Our Lord, she was sore amarvelled of her
visitation and thought herself far unworthy thereto,
and therefore said unto her, "Whereof is this, that the
mother of our Lord should come to me?"(Luke 1, 39-45).
But yet for all the abashment of her own unworthiness

she conceived thoroughly such a glad blessed comfort
that her holy child St John the Baptist leapt in her womb
for joy, whereof she said, "As soon as the voice of thy
salutation was in mine ears, the infant in my womb
leapt for joy." Now like as St Elizabeth by the Spirit
of God had those holy affections, both of reverent considering her own unworthiness in the visitation of the
mother of God, and yet for all that so great inward
gladness therewith, let us at this great high visitation,
in which not the mother of God, as came to St Elizabeth, but one incomparably more excelling the mother
of God than the mother of God passed St Elizabeth,
doth so vouchsafe to come and visit each of us with his
most blessed presence, that he cometh not into our
house but into ourself, let us, I say, call for the help of
the same Holy Spirit that then inspired her, and pray
him at this high and holy visitation so to inspire us that
we may both be abashed with the reverent dread of our
own unworthiness, and yet therewith conceive a joyful
consolation and comfort in the consideration of God's
inestimable goodness. And that each of us, like as we
may well say with great reverent dread and admiration
"Whereof is this, that my Lord should come unto me?"
And not only unto me but also into me; so we may
with glad heart truly say at the sight of his blessed
presence, "The child in my womb, that is to wit, the
soul in my body, that should be then such a child in
innocence, as was that innocent infant St John, leapeth
good Lord, for joy." *(1268)*

17. *Take from me, good Lord, this lukewarm fashion,
or rather key-cold manner of meditation and this dullness
in praying unto thee. And give me warmth, delight and
quickness in thinking upon thee. And give me thy grace
to long for thine holy sacraments, and specially to rejoice*

in the presence of thy very blessed body, sweet Saviour Christ, in the holy sacrament of the altar, and duly to thank thee for thy gracious visitation therewith, and at that high memorial, with tender compassion, to remember and consider thy most bitter passion. Make us all, good Lord, virtually participant of that holy sacrament this day, and every day make us all lively members, sweet Saviour Christ, of thine holy mystical body, thy Catholic Church. (1417)

18. And therefore wished I the last time after you were gone, when I felt myself, to say the truth, even a little weary, that I had not so told you still a long tale alone, but that we had more often interchanged words and parted the talk between us, with more interjection upon your part, in such manner as learned men use between the persons whom they devise disputing in their feigned dialogues. But yet in that point I soon excused you and laid the lack even where I found it, and that was even upon mine own neck. For I remembered that between you and me it fared as it did once between a nun and her brother. Very virtuous was this lady, and of a very virtuous place in a close religion, and therein had been long, in all which time she had never seen her brother, which was in likewise very virtuous too, and had been far off at an university, and had there taken the degree of doctor of divinity. When he was come home he went to see his sister as he that highly rejoiced in her virtue. So came she to the grate that they call, I believe, the locutory, and after their holy watch-word spoken on both sides, after the manner used in that place, the one took the other by the tip of the finger (for hand would there be none wrung through the grate) and forthwith began the lady to give her brother a sermon of the wretchedness of this world and the frailty of the flesh,

and the subtle sleights of the wicked fiend, and gave him surely good counsel, saving somewhat too long, how he should be well aware in his living, and master well his body for saving of his soul. And yet, ere her own tale came all at an end, she began to find a little fault with him and said, "In good faith, brother, I do somewhat marvel that you, that have been at learning so long, and are doctor, and so learned in the law of God, do not now at our meeting, while we meet so seldom, to me that am your sister and a simple unlearned soul, give of your charity some fruitful exhortation. And as I doubt not but you can say some good thing yourself." "By my troth, good sister," quoth her brother, "I can not for you. For your tongue hath never ceased but said enough for us both." *(1170)*

19. Howbeit, very long lasteth no man with the surfeits of gluttony. For undoubtedly nature, which is sustained with right little (as well appeared by the old fathers that so many years lived in the desert with herbs only and roots) is very sore oppressed, and in manner overwhelmed, and with the great weight and burden of much and divers viands, and so much laboureth to master the meat and to divide and separately to send it into all parts of the body and there to turn it into the like and retain it, that she is by force and great resistance of so much meat as she hath to work upon (of which every part laboureth to conserve and keep his own nature and kind such as it is) wearied and overcome and giveth it over, except it be helped by some outward aid. And this driveth us of necessity to have so much recourse to medicines, to pills, potions, plasters, clysters, and suppositaries; and yet all too little; our gluttony is so great and therewith so diverse that, while one meat digesteth, another lieth and putrefieth. And ever we

desire to have some help to keep the body in health. And when we be counselled to live temperately and forbear our delicacies and our gluttony, that will we not hear of, but fain would have some medicines as purgatives and vomits to pull down and void that we cram in too much. And in this we fare (as the great moral philosopher Plutarch saith) like a foolish master of a ship that goeth not about to see the ship tight and sure but letteth by his carelessness his ship fall on a leak, and then careth not yet to stop the chinks, but set more men to the pump rather with much travail and great peril to draw it dry, than with little labour and great surety to keep it dry. "Thus fare we," saith Plutarch, "that through intemperate living drive ourselves to sickness, and patch us up with physic, where we might with sober diet and temperance have less need of and keep ourselves in health." *(100)*

20. We be so wont to set so much by our body which we see and feel, and in the feeding and fostering thereof we set our delight and our wealth, and so little, alas!, and so seldom we think on our soul, because we cannot see that but by spiritual understanding, and most specially by the eye of our faith (in the meditation whereof we bestow, God knows, little time) that the loss of our body we take for a sorer thing and for a greater tribulation a great deal than we do for the loss of our soul. *(1181)*

21. For surely as touching the withdrawal of God's hand which his high goodness and unsearchable wisdom doth divers times, for more causes than men have the wit to spy, yet doth he it never but man withdraweth first his will. *(591)*

22. Lo, the holy doctor, St Austin, exhorting penitents and repentant sinners to sorrow for their offences, saith unto them, "Sorrow," saith this holy man, "and be glad of thy sorrow." In vain should he bid him be glad of his sorrow, if man in sorrow could not be glad. But this holy father showeth by this counsel not only that a man may be joyful and glad for all his sorrow, but also that he may be and hath cause to be glad because of his sorrow. Long were it to rehearse the places that prove this point among the holy doctors of Christ's Church, but we will instead of them all allege you the words of him that is doctor of them all, our Saviour Jesu Christ. He saith that the way to heaven is strait and narrow and painful. And therefore he saith that few folk find it out or walk therein. And yet saith he for all that, "My yoke is easy and my burden light" (Matt. 11, 30). How could these two sayings stand together were it not that as the labour, travail and affliction of the body is painful and sharp to the flesh, so the comfort and gladness that the soul conceiveth thereof, rising into the love of our Lord and hope of his glory to come, so tempereth and overmastereth the bitterness of the grief, that it maketh the very labour easy, the sourness very sweet, and the very pain pleasant? *(74)*

23. This fault of pusillanimity and timorous mind stoppeth a man also many times from the doing of many good things, which, if he took a good stomach to him in the trust of God's help, he were well able to do. But the devil casteth him in a cowardice and maketh him take it for humility, to think himself unmeet and unable thereto, and therefore to leave the good thing undone whereof God offereth him occasion and had made him fit and convenient thereto. But such folk have need to lift up their hearts and call upon God and by the counsel

of other good spiritual folk cast away the cowardice of their own conceit, and look in the Gospel upon him which laid up his talent and left it unoccupied, and therefore utterly lost it, with a great reproach of his pusillanimity by the which he had thought he should have excused himself, in that he was afeared to put it forth in use and occupy it. *(1182)*

24. But surely this worldly prosperity, wherein a man so rejoiceth and whereof the devil maketh him so proud, is but even a very short winter day. For we begin, many full poor and cold, and up we fly like an arrow that were shot up into the air; and yet when we be suddenly shot up into the highest, ere we be well warm there, down we come into the cold ground again and then even there stick we still. And yet for the short while that we be upward and aloft, Lord! how brave and how proud we, be buzzing above busily like as a bumble bee flieth about in summer, never aware that she shall die in winter. And so fare many of us, God help us! For in the short winter day of worldly wealth and prosperity this flying arrow of the devil, this high spirit of pride, shot out of the devil's bow and piercing through our heart, beareth us up in our affection aloft into the clouds, where we think we sit on the rainbow and overlook the world under us, accounting in the regard of our own glory such other poor souls as were peradventure wont to be our fellows, for foolish poor ants. *(1199)*

25. In such as are baptized young, the inward motion is the same goodness of God guiding them with the habitual faith infused in the sacrament of baptism. Upon the seed whereof with the help of God's grace, there springeth after in the good and well appliable will of man the fruit of credence and belief which they give

unto Christ's Catholic Church according to his own commandment upon the preaching of the same Church, in the reasons which the same Church by God's good ordinances giveth as outward means of credence and inducing to belief, both of itself and of the Scripture and of every part of the faith. *(705)*

26. Now in the study of Scripture, in looking for the sense, in considering what ye read, in pondering the purpose of divers comments, in comparing together divers texts that seem contrary and be not, albeit I deny not but that grace and God's especial help is the great thing therein, yet useth he for an instrument man's reason thereto. God helpeth us to eat also but yet not without our mouth. Now as the hand is the more nimble by the use of some feats, and the legs and feet more swift and sure by custom of going and running, and the whole body the more wieldly and active by some kind of exercise, so is it no doubt but that reason is by study, labour and exercise of logic, philosophy and other liberal arts strengthened and quickened and that judgment both in them, and also in orators, laws and stories much ripened. And albeit poets be with many men take but for painted words, yet do they much help the judgment, and make a man among other things well furnished of one special thing, without which all learning is half lame.

What is that? quod he.

Mary, quod I, a good mother wit. *(153)*

27. But when that whole kingdoms and mighty empires are of so little surety to stand, but be so soon translated from one man unto another, what great thing can you or I, yea, or any lord the greatest in this land, reckon himself to have by the possession of an

heap of silver or gold, white and yellow metal, not so profitable of their own nature save for a little glistering, as the rude rusty metal of iron? *(1219)*

28. Though faith be the first gate into heaven, he that standeth still at the gate and will not walk forth in the way of good works, shall not come where the reward is. *(1320)*

29. And yet, son Roper, I pray God that some of us, as high as we seem to sit upon the mountains, treading heretics under our feet like ants, live not the day that we gladly would wish to be at league and composition with them, to let them have their churches quietly to themselves so that they would be content to let us have ours quietly to ourselves. *(18*)*

30. If it so be that a man perceiveth that in wealth and authority he doth his own soul harm, and cannot do therein the good that to his part appertaineth, but seeth the things that he should set his hands to sustain decay through his default, and fall to ruin under him, and that to the amendment thereof he leaveth his own duty undone, then would I in anywise advise him to leave off that thing, be it spiritual benefice that he have, parsonage or bishopric, or temporal room and authority, and rather give it over quite, and draw himself aside and serve God, than take the worldly worship and convenience for himself, with disadvantage to them whom his duty were to profit. But on the other side, if he see not the contrary, that he may do his duty conveniently well, and feareth nothing, but that the temptations of ambition and pride may peradventure turn his good purpose and make him decline unto sin, I say not nay, but that well done it is to stand in moderate fear al-

way. whereof the Scripture saith, "Blessed is the man
that is alway fearful" (Prov. 28, 14), and St Paul saith
"He that standeth, let him look that he fall not" (I Cor.
10, 12). Yet is overmuch fear perilous and draweth
toward the mistrust of God's gracious help, which immoderate fear and faint heart Holy Scripture forbiddeth,
saying, "Be not feeble hearted or timorous" (Ecclus 7, 9).
(1200)

31. Though God invited men unto the following of
himself in wilful poverty, by the leaving of all together
at once for his sake, as the thing whereby with being out
of the solicitude of worldly business, and far from the
desire of earthly advantage, they may the more speedily
get and attain the state of spiritual perfection, and the
hungry desire and longing for celestial things—yet
doth he not command every man so to do upon the peril
of damnation. *(1205)*

SEPTEMBER

1. *O my sweet Saviour Christ, which in thine unde- served love towards mankind, so kindly wouldst suffer the painful death of the cross, suffer not me to be cold nor lukewarm in love again towards thee.* (1306)

2. For as it is a vice and some fault to be in the service of God superstitious instead of religious, over dreadful and scrupulous instead of devout and diligent, so is it a much more fault to be therein reckless and negligent. For accursed is he, as Holy Scripture saith, that doth the work of God negligently (Jer. 48, 10) *(208)*

3. For like as the good man in tribulation sent him by God, conformeth his will to God's will in that behalf, and giveth God thank therefore, so doth the wealthy man in his wealth which God giveth him conform his will to God's will in that point, since he is well content to take it of his gift, and giveth God again also right hearty thank therefor. *(1167)*

4. Zaccheus, lo, that climbed up into the tree for desire that he had to behold our Saviour, at such time as Christ called aloud unto him, "Zaccheus, make haste and come down, for this day must I dwell in thy house" (Luke 19, 5), was so glad thereof, and so touched inwardly with special grace to the profit of his soul, that whereas all the people murmured much that Christ would call him and be so familiar with him, as of his own offer to come into his house, considering that they knew him for the chief of the publicans, that were customers or toll-gatherers of the emperor's duties, all which whole

company were among the people sore accused of rapine extortion, and bribery, and then Zaccheus, not only the chief of that fellowship, but also grown greatly rich, whereby the people accounted him in their own opinion, for a man sinful and nought; he forthwith, by the instinct of the Spirit of God, in reproach of all such temerarious, bold and blind judgment given upon a man, whose inward mind and sudden change they cannot see, shortly proved them all deceived, and that our Lord had at those few words outwardly spoken to him, so touched him, that his grace so wrought in his heart within that whatsoever he was before, he was then, unaware unto them all, suddenly grown good. For he made haste and came down and gladly received Christ and said, "Lo, Lord, the one half of my good here I give unto poor people, and yet over that, if I have in any thing deceived any man, here am I ready to recompense him fourfold as much." *(1206)*

5. I have seen many vices were this that at the first seemed far from pride, and yet well considered to the uttermost it would well appear that of that root they sprang. As for wrath and envy they be the known children of pride, as rising of an high estimation of ourselves. But what would seem farther from pride than drunken gluttony? And yet shall ye find more that drink themselves sow drunk of pride to be called good fellows than for lust of the drink self. So spreadeth this cursed root of pride his branches into all other kinds besides his proper malice for his own part. *(82)*

6. I doubt not good readers but ye remember well that all the doctrine of Christ's Church is full of warning that no man should put a proud trust and confidence in his own works, nor once think that he can of himself alone

without God's gracious help do any good work at all, and great cause hath to fear and mistrust all his own works, for unperfect circumstances seldom perceived by himself. *(529)*

7. And verily in this declination of the world and by this great fall of faith, the old fervour of charity so beginning to cool, it is to be feared at length that if it thus go forth and continue, both the spirituality from the Apostles and the temporality from the other disciples, may fall so far down, down, down, down, that as there was then one nought among twelve, so may there in time coming if these heresies go forward, among twelve spiritual or peradventure twenty temporal either, be found at last in some whole country scant any one good. But that world is not, I thank God, in England yet, nor never shall I trust come. *(877)*

8. There is no greater riches, no greater treasures, no greater honours, nor no greater substance of this world, than is the Catholic faith which saveth sinful men and giveth to the blind their sight again, and healeth the sick, which also christeneth those that are new come to Christian religion and justifieth the faithful, repaireth penitents, increaseth the righteous folk, crowneth martyrs, giveth orders to the clergy, consecrateth priests, prepareth us to the kingdom of heaven and maketh us fellows and copartners with the holy angels in the everlasting inheritance. *(804)*

9. It is no mastery for you children to go to heaven, for everybody giveth you good counsel, everybody giveth you good example; you see virtue rewarded and vice punished, so that you are carried up to heaven even by the chins. But if you live the time that no man will

give you good counsel, nor no man will give you good example, when you shall see virtue punished and vice rewarded, if you will then stand fast and firmly stick to God, upon pain of my life, though you be but half good, God will allow you for the whole. *(14*)*

10. For surely this sin of pride, as it is the first of all sins, begun among the angels in heaven, so it is the head and root of all other sins and of them all most pestilent. *(1273)*

11. The Catholic Church teacheth that men should therefore put no proud trust in their merits but stand in fear of their unperfect working mingled alway for the most part with unperfection and spots, since that all the justice of man is, as the Scripture saith, like a foul spotted clout and that the stars are not clean in the eyes of God (Is. 64, 6; Job 25, 5). *(740)*

12. I fear me there be many folk that for delight of knowledge, or for a foolish vain glory to show and make it known how much themself know, labour to know the law of God, and know it right well indeed, and can well preach it out again, that shall yet see many a poor simple soul with a gross plain faith, with no learning but good devout affection, walking the way of good works in this world, sit after full high with our Lord in heaven, when these great clerks wandering here in evil works, shall for all their great knowledge, and for all gay preaching in the name of Christ, hear our Lord say to them, "Walk you from me you workers of wickedness." *(1320)*

13. There is not an old church of Christ and his apostles, and another new Church now, but one whole

Church from that time to this time in one true faith continued. *(654)*

14. Christ hath by his death paid every man's ransom and hath delivered us if we will, though many men there be that will not take the benefit thereof. But some will needs be still in prison, and some will needs thither again, as no man can keep some thieves out of Newgate; but let them be pardoned and their fees paid, and themselves set on free-foot and delivered out, yet will they there for good company tarry loose with their fellows awhile, and before that next Sessions come, sit as fast there as ever they sat before. *(743)*

15. Heretics be all they that obstinately hold any self-minded opinion contrary to the doctrine that the common known Catholic Church teacheth and holdeth for necessary to salvation. *(941)*

16. Now when we have received our Lord and have him in our body, let us not then let him alone, and get us forth about other things and look no more unto him (for little good could he that so would serve any guest) but let all our business be about him. Let us by devout prayer talk to him, by devout meditation talk with him. Let us say with the prophet, "I will hear what our Lord will speak within me" (Ps. 84, 9). For surely if we set aside all other things and attend unto him, he will not fail with good inspirations to speak such things to us within us as shall serve to the great spiritual comfort and profit of our soul. And therefore let us with Martha provide that all our outward business may be pertaining to him in making cheer to him and to his company for his sake, that is to wit, to poor folk of which he taketh every one, not only for his disciple, but also as for him-

self. For himself saith, "That that you have done to one
of the least of these my brethren, you have done it to
myself" (Matt. 25, 40). And let us with Mary also sit in
devout meditation and harken well what our Saviour,
being now our guest, will inwardly say unto us. Now
have we a special time for prayer, while he that hath
made us, he that hath bought us, he whom we have
offended, he that shall judge us, he that shall either damn
us or save us, is of his great goodness become our guest
and is personally present within us, and that for no other
purpose but to be sued unto for pardon and so thereby to
save us. Let us not lose this time therefore, suffer not
this occasion to slip, which we can little tell whether ever
we shall get it again or never. Let us endeavour ourself
to keep him still, and let us say with his two disciples
that were going to the castle at Emmaus, "Tarry with
us, Lord" (Luke 24, 29): and then shall we be sure that
he will not go from us, but if we unkindly put him from
us. Let us not pray like the people of Genesareth, which
prayed him to depart out of their quarters, because they
lost their hogs by him, when instead of hogs he saved
the man, out of whom he cast the legion of devils that
after destroyed the hogs. Let not us likewise rather put
God from us by unlawful love of worldly winning, or
foul filthy lust, rather than for the profit of our soul to
forbear it. For sure may we be that when we wax such,
God will not tarry with us, but we put him unkindly
from us. Nor let us not do as the people of Jerusalem,
which on Palm Sunday received Christ royally and full
devoutly in procession, and on Friday after put him to a
shameful passion. On the Sunday cried, "Blessed be he
that cometh in the name of the Lord" (Matt. 21, 9), and
on the Friday cried out, "We will not have him but
Barabbas!" (John 18, 40). On the Sunday cried, "Ho-
sanna in the highest!"; on the Friday, "Away with

him! Away with him! Crucify him!" (John 19, 15). Sure if we receive him never so well, nor never so devoutly at Easter, yet whensoever we fall after to such wretched sinful living, as casteth our Lord in such wise out of our souls, as his grace tarrieth not with us, we show ourself to have received him in such manner as those Jews did. For we do as much as in us is to crucify Christ again; saith St Paul, "Again crucifying the son of God" (Heb. 6, 6). *(1268)*

17. *Almighty God, have mercy on all that bear me evil will, and would me harm, and their faults and mine together by such easy, tender, merciful means, as thine infinite wisdom best can devise, vouchsafe to amend and redress and make us saved souls in heaven together where we may ever live and love together with thee and thy blessed saints. O glorious Trinity, for the bitter passion of our sweet Saviour Christ. Lord, give me patience in tribulation and grace in everything to conform my will to thine, that I may truly say, "Thy will be done on earth as it is in heaven." The things, good Lord, that I pray for, give me grace to labour for. Amen. (1418)*

18. So must reason not resist faith but walk with her, and as her handmaid wait upon her, that as contrary as ye take her, yet of a truth faith goeth never without her. But likewise as if a maid suffered to run on the bridle, or be inebriated, or grow too proud, she will then grow copious and chop logic with her masters, and fare sometimes as she were frantic : so if reason be suffered to run out at riot, and grow over high-hearted and proud, she will not fail to fall in rebellion towards her master's faith. But on the other side, if she be well brought up and well-guided and kept in good temper, she shall never disobey faith, being in her right mind. And there-

fore let reason be well guided, for surely faith goeth never without her. *(153)*

19. But some men now, when this calling of God causeth them to be sad, they be loth to leave their sinful lusts that hang in their hearts and specially if they have any such kind of living as they must needs leave off, or fall deeper into sin; or if they have done so many great wrongs that they have many mends to make, that must, if they follow God, diminish much their money, then are these folks, alas!, wofully rapt. For God worketh upon them of his great goodness still, and the grief of this great pang pincheth them at the heart, and of wickedness they wry away, and from this tribulation they turn to their flesh for help, and labour to shake off this thought, and then they mend their pillow, and lay their head softer, and essay to sleep; and when that will not be, then they find a talk awhile with them that lie by them. If that cannot be neither, then they lie and long for day, and then get them forth about their worldly wretchedness the matter of their prosperity, the selfsame sinful things with which they displease God most, and at length with many times using this manner God utterly casteth them off. And then they set nought neither by God nor devil. *(1161)*

20. Men of substance must there be, for else shall you have more beggars, assuredly, than there be, and no man left able to relieve another. For this I think in my mind a very sure conclusion, that if all the money that is in this country were to-morrow next brought together out of every man's hand, and laid all upon one heap, and then divided out unto every man alike, it would be on the morrow after worse than it was the day before. For I suppose when it were all equally thus divided among

all, the best should be left little better then than almost a beggar is now. And yet he that was a beggar before, all that he shall be the richer for that he should thereby receive, shall not make him much above a beggar still, but many one of the rich men, if their riches stood but in movable substance, shall be safe enough from riches haply for all their life after. *(1208)*

21. Though I be bounden to give every manner man in some manner of his necessity, were he my friend or my foe, Christian man or heathen, yet am I not unto all men bounden alike, nor unto any man in every case alike. The differences of the circumstances make great change in the matter. St Paul saith, "He that provideth not for those that are his, is worse than an infidel" (1 Tim. 5, 8). Those are ours that are belonging to our charge, either by nature, or law, or any commandment of God. By nature, as our children; by law, as our servants in our household. So that albeit these two sorts be not ours all alike, yet would I think that the least ours of the twain, that is to wit, our servants, if they need and lack, we be bounden to look to them, and provide for their need, and see so far forth as we may, that they lack not the things that should serve for their necessity while they dwell in our service. Meseemeth also that if they fall sick in our service, so that they cannot do the service that we retain them for, yet may we not in any wise turn them then out of doors, and cast them up comfortless while they be not able to labour and help themself, for this were a thing against all humanity. *(1208)*

22. And thus finish I this matter concerning heresies, beseeching our Lord and Saviour for his bitter passion, that as his holy sacraments thereof took their strength, so by the prayer of all those holy saints that have both

by their holy doctrine and example of living, some of
them planted the faith, and some of them in sundry
times well watered the plants, so himself will by his
goodness specially now vouchsafe as the warm son (the
very eternal only begotten Son of his eternal Father) to
spread his beams upon us, and aspire his breath into us,
and in our hearts, as St Paul saith, give his faith strength
and increase (1 Cor. 3, 6). *(926)*

23. But God is more merciful to man's imperfection
if the man know it and acknowledge it and mislike it and
little by little labour to mend it, than to reject and cast
off to the devil him that after as his frailty can bear and
suffer, hath a general intent and purpose to please him,
and to prefer or set by nothing in all this world before
him. *(1210)*

24. The fellowship of the saints, that is to say, let us
hold ourself in the communion and fellowship of hope
with those saints which are deceased in this faith which
we have received. Therefore if we will have fellowship
with the saints in the everlasting life, let us think upon
the following of them. For they must recognize and find
in us somewhat of their virtues to the intent they may
vouchsafe to pray for us unto our Lord. *(805)*

25. To such wretches as care not for their conscience
but like unreasonable beasts follow their foul affections,
many of these temptations be no trouble at all, but
matter of bodily pleasure. But into him that standeth
in dread of God, the tribulation of temptation is so
painful that to be rid thereof, or sure of the victory
therein (be his substance never so great), he would
gladly give more than half. *(1158)*

26. And they tell us that we shall be damned but if we believe right, and then tell us that we cannot know that but by the Scripture and that the Scripture cannot be so learned but by a true teacher, and they tell us we cannot be sure of a true teacher, and so cannot be sure to understand it right, and yet say that God will damn us for understanding it wrong, or not understanding at all. They that thus tell us put me in mind of a tale that they tell of Master Henry Patenson [1], a man of known wisdom in London and almost everywhere else, which when he waited once on his master in the Emperor's Court at Bruges and was there soon perceived upon the sight for a man of special wit by himself and unlike the common sort, they caught a sport in angering of him and out of divers corners hurled at him such things as angered him and hurt him not. Thereupon he gathered up good stones, not gunstones but as hard as they, and those he put within his bosom, and then stood him up upon a bench and made a proclamation aloud that every man might hear him, in which he commanded every man upon his own perils to depart except only those that hurled at him, to the intent that he might know them again and hurt none other body but his enemies. For whosoever tarried after his proclamation made, he would take for one of the hurlers or else for one of their counsellors and then have at their heads whoever they were that would abide. Now was his proclamation in English and the company that heard him were such as understood none and gaped upon him and laughed at him. And by and by one hurled at him again. And anon as he saw that, "What, whoresons," quoth he, "ye stand still everyone I see and not one of you will remove a foot for my proclamation, and thereby I see well ye be hurlers or of council with the hurlers, all the whole main of you,

---

[1] More's family jester; August 1521 when More was on an embassy.

and therefore have at you all again." And with the word
he hurled a great stone out at adventure among them,
he neither knew nor recked at whom, but lighted upon a
Burgundian's head and break his pate that the blood
ran about his ears, and Master Henry bad him stand to
his harness hardly, for why would he not beware then
and get hence betime, when he gave him before so fair
courteous warning. *(768)*

27. If we should see two men fighting together for
very great things, yet would we reckon them both mad
if they left not off when they should see a ramping lion
coming on them both, ready to devour them both. Now
when we see surely that death is coming on us all and
shall undoubtedly within a short space devour us all,
and how soon know not all, is it not now more than
madness to be wroth and bear malice one to another, and
for the more part for as very trifles as children should
fall at variance for cherrystones, death coming, as I
say, upon us to devour us all? *(88)*

28. Let every man fear and think in this world that
all the good that he doth, or can do, is a great deal too
little. *(1210)*

29. Two things seem to me two as true points and as
plain to a Christian man as any proposition of Euclid's
geometry is to a reasonable man. For as true as it is that
every whole thing is more than his own half, as true as it
indeed and to every Christian man faith maketh it as
certain—First, that Christ's Church cannot err in any
such article as God upon pain of loss of heaven will that
we believe. And thereupon necessarily followeth that
there is no text of Scripture well understanden by which
Christian people are commanded to do the thing which

the Church believeth that they may lawfully leave un-done, nor any text whereby we be forboden any thing which the Church believeth that they may lawfully do. *(149)*

30. If the whole world were animated with a reason-able soul, as Plato had thought it were, and that it had wit and understanding to mark and perceive all thing, Lord God! how the ground on which a prince buildeth his palace would loud laugh his lord to scorn when he saw him proud of his possession and heard him boast himself that he and his blood are for ever the very lords and owners of that land! For then would the ground think the while in himself, "Ah, thou foolish poor soul, that thinkest thou were half a god and art amid thy glory but a man in a gay gown, I that am the ground here, over whom thou art so proud, have had an hundred such owners of me as thou callest thyself, more than ever thou hast heard the names of. And some of them that proudly went over mine head, lie now low in my belly, and my side lieth over them. And many one shall, as thou dost now, call himself mine owner after thee that neither shall be kin to thy blood nor any word hear of thy name." *(1219)*

OCTOBER

1. *Almighty Jesus Christ, which wouldst for our example observe the law that thou camest to change, and being maker of the whole earth wouldst have yet no dwelling house therein, give us thy grace so to keep thine holy law and so to reckon ourselves for no dwellers but for pilgrims upon earth, that we may long and make haste, walking with faith in the way of virtuous works, to come to the glorious country wherein thou hast bought us inheritance for ever with thine own precious blood. (1313)*

2. If a lewd priest do a lewd deed, then we say, lo, see what example the clergy giveth us, as though that priest were the clergy. But then we forget to look what good men be therein, and what good counsel they give us, and what good example they show us. But we fare as do the ravens and the carrion crows that never meddle with any quick flesh, but where they may find a dead dog in a ditch, thereto they flee and thereon they feed apace. So where we see a good man and hear and see a good thing, there we take little heed. But when we see once an evil deed, thereon we gape, thereof we talk, and feed ourselves all day with the filthy delight of evil communication. Let a good man preach, a short tale shall serve us thereof and we shall neither much regard his exhortation nor his good examples. But let a lewd friar be taken with a wench, we will jest and rail upon the whole order all the year after and say, lo, what example they give us. And yet, when we have said, we will follow the same and then say we learned it of them, forgetting that we please not to hear and follow some other whose word and deed would give us light to do better, if we

chose as well to learn the better as to follow the worse.
(225)

3. And yet are there some fools so, fed with this fond fantasy of fame that they rejoice and glory to think how they be continually praised all about, as though all the world did nothing else day nor night but ever sit and sing, "Sanctus, sanctus, sanctus," upon them. *(1221)*

4. Of spiritual counsel, the first is to be shriven [confessed], that by reason of his other sins the devil have not the more power upon him. *(1197)*

5. Now if a man willingly kill himself with a knife, the world wondereth thereupon, and, as well worthy is, he is indicted of his own death, his goods forfeited and his corpse cast out on a dunghill, his body never buried in Christian burail. These gluttons daily kill themselves with their own hands and no man findeth fault, but carrieth his carrion corpse into the choir, and with much solemn service burieth the body boldly at the high altar, when they have all their life (as the apostle saith) made their belly their God and liked to know no other, abusing not only the name of Christian men, preferring their belly joy before all the joys of heaven, but also abusing the part and office of a natural man and reasonable creature. For whereas nature and reason showeth us that we should eat but for to live, these gluttons are so glutted in the beastly pleasure of their taste that they would not wish to live an it were not for to eat. But surely wisdom were it for these gluttons well and effectually to consider that, as St Paul saith, "The meat for the belly and the belly to the meat; but God shall destroy both the meat and the belly" (1 Cor. 6, 13). *(100)*

6. In all that a man may do, he doeth but his only duty, and that the best work were nought worth to heavenward of the nature of the work itself, nor were it for the liberal goodness of God that listeth so highly to reward it, and yet would not reward it so saving for the passion of his own Son. All these things, and many such other more, be so daily taught and preached in the Church that I trust in good faith that almost every good wife can tell them. *(529)*

7. Howbeit this one thing, son, I assure thee on my faith, that if the parties will at my hands call for justice, then, all were it my father stood on the one side and the devil on the other, his cause being good, the devil should have right. *(12*)*

8. Therefore my dearest brethren, although we suffer no such thing, no bonds, no stripes, no emprisonment, none other bloody torments, nor no persecution of men for righteousness sake, yet we may be able to obtain the fellowship of the saints if we labour and chastise our body and make it subject, if we accustom ourselves to pray unto our Lord with an humble spirit and contrite soul, if we endeavour ourself to take with a peaceable mind the slights that are done unto us by our neighbour, if we contend and strive with ourself to love those that hate us and do us wrong and do to them good and to pray gladly for their life and welfare, and to be with the virtue of patience and the fruits of good works, garnished and made gay. *(805)*

9. For I think that every man's duty toward God is so great, that very few folk serve him as they should do. And therefore whoso pry upon every man's deed so narrowly, as to spy that fault and fall at variance of great

zeal with every man that doth not to the very point and perfection, even all that he should do, shall grow within a while at variance with every man and every man with him. *(876)*

10. Where sin hath abounded, there hath grace also more abounded that likewise as sin hath reigned unto death, so grace should also reign by justice unto everlasting life through Jesus Christ our Lord. *(1283)*

11. Both may a man have the right faith idle and workless and therefore dead and fruitless. Dead I say not in the nature and substance of belief and faith, but dead as to the attaining salvation. *(529)*

12. For every man learned and unlearned for so far as toucheth the necessary doctrine of true faith and living and exposition of the Scripture that appertaineth thereto, the very fastness and surety is, to rest unto the Church which is, as St Paul saith, the pillar and sure ground of truth (1 Tim. 3, 15). *(658)*

13. He made me therewith remember a like matter of a man of mine seven year afore, one Davy, a Dutchman, which had been married in England and saying that his wife was dead and buried at Worcester two year before, while he was in his country and giving her much praise and often telling us how sorry he was when he came home and found her dead, and how heavily he had made her bitter prayers at her grave, went about while he waited upon me at Bruges [1] in the King's business to marry there an honest widow's daughter. And so happened it that even upon the day when they should have been made handfast and ensured together, was I

---

[1] August 1521. See, 26 Sep. above.

advertised from London by my wife's letter, that
David's wife was alive and had been at my house to seek
him. Whereupon I called him before me and other and
read the letter to him. "Marry, master", quoth he,
"that letter saith methink that my wife is alive." "Yes,
beast," quoth I, "that she is." "Marry," quoth he,
"then I am well apaid, for she is a good woman." "Yea,"
quoth I, "but why art thou such a naughty wretched
man that thou wouldst here wed another? Didst thou
not say she was dead?" "Yes, marry, good men of
Worcester told me so." "Why," quoth I, "thou false
beast, didst not thou tell me and all my house that thou
were at her grave thyself?" *(718)*

14. We say that God rejoiceth and delighteth in the
love of man's heart when he findeth it such as the man
inwardly delighteth in his heart, and outwardly to let the
love of his heart so redound into the body that he gladly by fasting and other affliction putteth the body to
pain for God's sake, and yet thinketh for all that, that
in comparison of his duty all that is much less than right
nought. *(372)*

15. Now where ye say that ye see more vice in the
clergy than in ourself, truth it is that everything in them
is greater because they be more bounden to be better.
But else, the things that they misdo be the selfsame that
we sin in ourself, which vices that as ye say we see more
in them than in ourself, the cause is I suppose, for we
look more upon theirs than on our own, and fare as
Æsop saith in the fable that every man carrieth a double
wallet on his shoulder, and into the one that hangeth
at his breast he putteth other folks' faults and therein
he peereth and poreth often. In the other he layeth up
all his own and swingeth it at his back, which himself

never troubleth to look in, but other that come after him cast an eye into it among. Would God we were all of the mind that every man thought no man so bad as himself. For that were to mend both them and us. *(225)*

16. Let us, good Christian readers, receive Christ in such wise as did the good publican Zaccheus, which when he longed to see Christ, and because he was but low in stature, did climb up into a tree. (Luke 19). Our Lord seeing his devotion called unto him and said, "Zaccheus, come off and come down, for this day must I dwell with thee". And he made haste and came down and very gladly received him into his house. But not only received him with a joy of a light and soon sliding affection, but that it might well appear that he received him with a sure earnest virtuous mind, he proved it by his virtuous works. For he forthwith was contented to make recompense to all men that he had wronged, and that in a large manner, for every penny a fourpenny-piece; and yet offered to give out also forthwith the one half of all his substance unto the poor men, and that forthwith also, straightway, without any longer delay. And therefore he said not, "Thou shalt hear that I shall give it", but he said, "Lo, look, good Lord, the one half on my goods I do give unto poor men." With such alacrity, with such quickness of spirit, with such gladness, and such spiritual rejoicing, as this man received our Lord into his house, our Lord give us the grace to receive his blessed body and blood, his holy soul, and his almighty godhead, both into our bodies and into our souls, that the fruit of our good works may bear witness unto our conscience that we receive him worthily and in such a full faith, and such a stable purpose of good living, as we be bounden to do. And then shall God give a gracious sentence and say unto our soul, as he said upon

Zaccheus, "This day is health and salvation come unto this house", which that holy blessed person Christ, which we verily in the blessed sacrament receive, through the merit of his bitter passion—whereof he hath ordained his only blessed body, in that blessed sacrament, to be the memorial—vouchsafe, good Christian readers, to grant unto us all. *(1269)*

17. And thus I beseech our Lord to send us everyone, both the spiritual and the temporal too, both wit and grace to agree together in goodness, and each to love other, and each for other to pray, and for those that by both parts are passed into purgatory, and there pray for us as we here pray for them, that they and we both through the merits of Christ's bitter passion, may both with our own prayers and the intercession of all holy saints in heaven, avoiding the eternal fire of hell, have pity poured upon us in the very fire of purgatory, which in those two places verily burneth souls. And finally for our faith and good works which his grace (working with the wills of those that wit have) giveth each good man here, God give us in heaven together everlasting glory. *(1034)*

18. I would that we were all in case with our own faults as my father saith that we be with our wives. For when he heareth folk blame wives and say that there be so many of them shrews, he saith that they defame them falsely. For he saith plainly that there is but one shrewd wife in the world, but he saith indeed that every man believeth he hath her, and that that one is his own. So would I fain that every man would know that there were but one man nought in the whole world and that that one were himself. And that he would thereupon go about to mend the one, and thus would all grow well, which

thing we should shortly do if we would once turn our wallet that I told you of [*15 Oct.*] and the bag with other folk's faults cast at our back, and cast the bag that beareth our own faults, cast it once before us at our breast; it would be a goodly thing for us to look on our own faults another while. And I dare boldly say, both they and we should much the better amend if we were so ready each to pray for other as we be ready to seek each other's reproach and rebuke. *(233)*

19. Men cannot, you know well, live here in this world but if some one man provide a mean of living for some other many. Every man cannot have a ship of his own, nor every man be a merchant without a stock, and these things, you know well, must needs be had; every man cannot have a plough by himself. And who might live by the tailor's craft, if no man were able to put a gown to make? Who by the masonry or who could live a carpenter if no man were able to build neither a church nor house? Who should be makers of any manner cloth, if there lacked men of substance to set sundry sorts a work? Some man that hath but two ducats in his house were better forbear them both and leave himself not a farthing but utterly lose all his own, than that some rich man, by whom he is weekly set to work, should of his money lose the one half, for then were himself like to lack work. For surely the rich man's substance is the wellspring of the poor man's living. And therefore here would it fare by the poor man as it fared by the woman in one of Æsop's fables, which had an hen that laid her every day a golden egg, till on a day she thought she would have a great many eggs at once and therefore she killed her hen, and found but one or twain in her belly, so that for covetise of those few, she lost many. *(1208)*

20. I can well allow that men should commend, keeping them within the bonds of truth, such things as they see praiseworthy in other men, to give them the greater courage to the increase thereof. For men keep still in that point one condition of children, that praise must prick them forth, but better it were to do well and look for none. Howbeit, they that cannot find in their heart to commend another man's good deed, show themself either envious or else of nature very cold and dull. But out of question, he that putteth his pleasure in the praise of the people hath but a fond fantasy. For if his finger do but ache of an hot blain, a great many men's mouths blowing out his praise, will hardly do him among them all half so much ease, as to have one boy blow upon his finger. *(1223)*

21. Let us now consider what great worldly wealth ariseth unto men by great offices, rooms and authority; to those worldly-disposed people, I say, that desire them for no better purpose. The great thing that they chief like therein is that they may bear rule, command and control other men, and live uncommanded and un-controlled themself. And yet this advantage took I so little heed of that I never was ware it was so great, till a good friend of ours merrily told me once that his wife once in a great anger taught it him. For when her husband had no wish to grow greatly upward in the world, nor neither would labour for office of authority and over that forsook a right worshipful position when it was offered him, she fell in hand with him, he told me, and all too rated him, and asked him, "What will you do that you choose not to put forth yourself as other folks do? Will you sit still by the fire and make goslings in the ashes with a stick as children do? Would God I were a man, and look what I would do!" "Why, wife," quoth

her husband, "what would you do?" "What? By God! go forward with the best. For as my mother was wont to say (God have mercy on her soul!) it is ever better to rule than to be ruled. And therefore, by God, I would not I warrant you, be so foolish to be ruled where I might rule." "By my troth, wife," quoth her husband, "in this, I dare say, you say truth, for I never found you willing to be ruled yet". *(1224)*

22. Let a man reckon his years that are passed of his age ere ever he can get up aloft, and let him when he hath it first in his fist, reckon how long he shall be like to live after, and I am sure that then the most part shall have little cause to rejoice, they shall see the time likely to be so short that their honour and authority by nature shall endure, beside the manifold chances whereby they may lose it more soon. And then when they see that they must needs leave it, the thing which they did much set their heart upon, than ever they had reasonable cause; what sorrow they take therefor, that shall I not need to tell you. *(1225)*

23. For if our conversation be such and if we also according to the saying of the apostle exhibit our bodies a lively host, holy and pleasant unto God (Rom. 12, 1), we shall be gifted with the heavenly honour that we may be in one glory rewarded with them that for our Lord's sake gave their members to the death. *(805)*

24. The Church also doth not precisely bind any man to the belief of every thing written in a legend, as though every saint's legend were part of the Scripture of God. *(678)*

25. And in these means like as God useth the bodily senses which we call the five wits as ways and means toward that understanding when men attain by reason, though there be sometime between the reason and the bodily senses some debate and variance, so doth he use both the service of the bodily senses and of the reason of the soul toward the service of the faith, adding therewith, because it is a thing far above the nature of them both, his supernatural aid and help of his supernal grace to present us with occasions and motions of belief, and walking on with us, except we leave ourself to the perfecting of belief in our hearts, and helping us to incline our minds with the credence of those outward causes and motives which without his help in things ordained of God for the way heavenward, we should not have done, nor of God's ordinary course we should not have behaved without some such outward sensible causes neither as is preaching and miracles and some such other. *(694)*

26. This holy sacrament of matrimony was begun by God in Paradise and he there instituted it to signify the conjunction between himself and man's soul, and the conjunction between Christ and his Church. Yet in that coupling of matrimony (if they couple in him) he coupleth himself also to their souls, with grace, according to the sign, that is to say the which he hath set to signify that grace, and with that grace if they apply to work therewith, he helpeth them to make their marriage honourable and their bed undefiled. And with that grace also he helpeth them toward the good education and bringing up of such children as shall come between them. *(378)*

27. This manner of ours in whose breasts the great

good counsel of God no better settleth nor taketh no better root, may well declare us that the thorns and the briers and the brambles of our worldly substance grow so thick and spring so high in the ground of our hearts that they strangle, as the Gospel saith, the word of God that was sown therein. And therefore is God very good Lord unto us when he causeth like a good husbandman his folk to come into the field (for the persecutors be his folk to this purpose) and with their hooks and grub up these wicked weeds and bushes of our earthly substance, and carry them quite away from us that the word of God sown in our hearts may have room therein and a glade round about for the warm sun of grace to come in it and make it grow. *(1233)*

28. The great horror and fear that our Saviour had in his own flesh against his painful passion, maketh me little to marvel. And I may well make you take that comfort too, that for no such manner of reluctance felt in your sensual parts, the flesh shrinking at the meditation of pain and death, your reason shall give over, but resist it and manly master it. And though you would fain flee from the painful death and be loath to come thereto, yet may the meditation of his great grievous agony move you, and himself shall, if you so desire him, not fail to work with you therein, and get and give you the grace that you shall submit and conform your will therein unto his as he did unto his Father. *(1235)*

29. For since we be by our faith very sure that Holy Scripture is the very word of God, and that the word of God cannot be but true, and that we see that by the mouth of his holy prophet, and by the mouth of his blessed apostle also, God hath made us so faithful promise, both that he will not suffer us to be tempted

above our power, but will both provide a way out for us, and that he will also round so compass us with his shield and defend us that we shall have no cause to fear this midday devil with all his persecution. *(1236)*

30. And therefore while we be not in error of understanding and faith how so ever we fall, or how often so ever we sin, we see the way to turn again by grace to God's mercy. *(144)*

31. And like as it is in physic a special thing necessary to know where and in what place of the body lieth the beginning, and, as it were, the fountain of the sore from which the matter is always ministered unto the place where it appeareth (for the fountain once stopped, the sore shall soon heal of itself, the matter failing that fed it; which continually resorting from the fountain to the place, men may well daily purge and cleanse the sore but they shall hardly heal it) likewise, I say, fareth it by the sore of the soul; if we perceive once the root and dig up that, we be very sure the branches be surely gone. But while the root remaineth, while we cut off the branches, we let well the growing and keep it somewhat under, but fail they may not always to spring again. And therefore, since this ungracious branch of wrath springeth out of the cursed root of pride and setting much by ourselves, so secretly lurking in our heart that hardly we can perceive it ourselves, let us pull up well the root and surely the branch of wrath shall soon wither away. For taken once away the setting by ourselves, we shall not greatly dote upon that we set little by. So shall there of such humility, contempt and abjection of ourselves shortly follow in us high estimation, honour and love of God, and every other creature in order for his sake, as they shall appear more or less dear unto him. *(87)*

NOVEMBER

1. *Almighty Jesus, my sweet Saviour Christ, which wouldst vouchsafe thine own almighty hands to wash the feet of thy twelve apostles, not only of the good but of the very traitor too, vouchsafe, good Lord, of thine excellent goodness, in such wise to wash the foul feet of mine affections, that I never have such pride enter into mine heart as to disdain either in friend or foe, with meekness and charity for the love of thee, to defile mine hands with washing of their feet. (1320)*

2. For if that we because we know our cause so good, bear ourself thereupon so bold that we make light and slight of our adversaries, it may happen to fare between the Catholics and the heretics at length as it fareth sometime in a suit at law by some good man against whom a subtle wily knave beginneth a false action and asketh from him all the land he hath. This good man sometime that knoweth his matter so true persuadeth to himself that it were not possible for him to lose it by law. And when his counsel talketh with him and asketh him how he can prove this point or that, for himself answereth again, "Fear ye not for that, sir, I warrant you all the whole country knoweth it, the matter is so true, and my part so plain, that I care not what judges, what arbitrators, what twelve men go thereon. I will challenge no man for any labour that mine adversary can make therein." And with such good hope the good man goeth him home and there sitteth still and putteth no doubt in the matter. But in the meanwhile his adversary (which for lack of truth of his cause must needs put all his trust in craft) goeth about his matter busily and

by all the false means he may make him friends some with good fellowship, some with rewards, findeth him a fellow to forge him false evidence, maketh means to the sheriff, getteth a partial panel, laboureth the jury, and when they come to the bar he hath all his trinkets ready, whereas good Tom Truth cometh forth upon the other side, and because he believeth all the world knoweth how true his matter is, bringeth never a witness with him and all his evidence unsorted. And surely much after this fashion in many places play these heretics and we. For like as a few birds alway chirping and flying from bush to bush many times seem a great many, so these heretics be so busy walking, that in every ale house, in every tavern, in every barge, and almost every boat, as few as they be a man shall always find some, and there be they so busy with their talking and in better places also where they may be heard, so fervent and importune in putting forth of any thing which may serve for the furtherance of their purpose that between their importune pressing and the diligence or rather the negligence of good Catholic men, appeareth often times as great a difference as between frost and fire. And surely between the true Catholic folk and the false heretics, it fareth also much like as it fared between false Judas and Christ's faithful apostles. For while they for all Christ's calling upon them to wake and pray fell first in a slumber and after in a dead sleep, the traitor neither slept nor slumbered but went about full busily to betray his master and bring himself to mischief. But yet when he came with his company, they escaped not all scot free, nor Peter well awaked out of his sleep was not so slothful, but that he could cut off one of the knaves ear, nor all the wretches of them with all their weapons able to stand against Christ's bare word, when he said, "I am he whom ye seek", but to ground they fell forth-

with up right upon their backs (John 18, 6). Whereby
we be sure that neither heretics nor devils can anything
do but by God's special sufferance and that they shall
between them both never be able to destroy the Catholic faith, nor to prevail against the Catholic Church
and all the mischief shall be their own at length, though
God for our sin suffer them for a scourge to prevail in
some places here and there for a while whom upon
men's amendment he will not fail to serve at the last as
doth the tender mother which when she hath beaten
her child for his wantonness, wipeth his eyes and kisseth
him and casteth the rod in the fire. *(921)*

3. For no more is our faith sufficient of itself, but the
sufficiency thereof is also of God in that our Lord with
our endeavour giveth us grace to believe and in that it
liketh our Lord of his goodness so highly to reward it.
For surely as it is very true that St Paul saith, "All that
ever we can suffer in this world is not worthy the glory
to come that shall be shewed us" (Rom. 8, 18). For what
thing could a silly wretched creature do or suffer for God
in the brief time of this short life that might of right
require to be rewarded everlastingly, with such inestimable joy as neither eye hath seen, nor tongue can
express, nor heart can imagine or conceive? So is it also
as true that all the faith we have, or can have, can of his
own nature as little or much less deserve heaven as our
other good deeds. For what great thing do we to God,
or what great thing could we ask him of right because
we believe him, as though he were much beholden unto
us in that we vouchsafe to trust him, as though his
worship hung in our hands, and his estimation lost if he
were out of credence with us? *(270)*

4. Give God the thank and not me, for that work is his

and not mine. For neither am I able any good thing to say but by him, nor all the good words in this world, no not the holy words of God himself, and spoken also with his own holy mouth, can be able to profit the man with the sound entering at his ear, but if the Spirit of God therewith inwardly work in his soul. But that is his goodness ever ready to do, except the obstacle be through the untowardness of our own froward will. (*1237*)

5. If thou shouldst perceive that one were earnestly proud of the wearing of the gay golden gown while the rogue playeth the lord in a stage play, wouldst thou not laugh at his folly considering that thou art sure that when the play is done he shall go walk a knave in his old coat? Now thou thinkest thyself wise enough while thou art proud in thy player's garment, and forgettest that when thy play is done, thou shalt go forth as poor as he. Nor thou remembrest not that thy pageant may happen to be done as soon as his. (*83*)

6. Our Saviour was himself taken prisoner for our sake, and prisoner was he carried, and prisoner was he kept, and prisoner was he brought before Annas, and prisoner from Annas carried unto Caiphas, then prisoner was he carried from Caiphas unto Pilate, and prisoner was he sent from Pilate to King Herod, prisoner from Herod unto Pilate again, and so kept as prisoner to the end of his passion. The time of his imprisonment, I grant well, was not long; but as for hard handling, which our hearts must abhor, he had as much in that short while as many men among them all in much longer time. And surely, then, if we consider of what estate he was, and therewith that he was prisoner in such wise for our sake, we shall I am sure, but if we be worse than wretched beasts, never so shamefully

play the unkind cowards as for fear of imprisonment sinfully to forsake him, nor so foolish neither as by forsaking of him to give him the occasion again to forsake us, and with the avoiding of an easier prison, fall into a worse, and instead of prison that cannot keep us long, shall into that prison, out of which we can never come, whereas the short imprisonment would win us everlasting liberty. *(1248)*

7. I knew a woman once that came into a prison to visit of her charity a poor prisoner there whom she found in a chamber, to say the truth, fair enough, and at the leastwise it was strong enough. But with mats of straw the prisoner had made it so warm, both under the foot and round about the walls, that in these things for the keeping of his health she was on his behalf glad and very well comforted. But among many other displeasures that for his sake she was sorry for, one she lamented much in her mind, that he should have the chamber door upon him by night made fast by the jailer that should shut him in. "For by my troth," quoth she, "if the door should be shut upon me, I believe it would stop up my breath." At that word of hers the prisoner laughed in his mind, but he durst not laugh aloud nor say nothing to her, for somewhat indeed he stood in awe of her, and had his support there much part of her charity for alms, but he could not but laugh inwardly, while he knew well enough that she used on the inside to shut every night full surely her own chamber to her, both door and windows too, and used not to open them of all the long night. And what difference then, as to the stopping of the breath, whether they were shut up within or without? *(1247)*

8. There shall ever be in this world both corn and

chaff and straw, and in Christ's net in the sea of this
world there shall never lack bad fish among the good,
and in Christ's field here upon earth there shall never
lack cockle among the corn. And yet shall it still be
Christ's holy church and his holy field, so holy ,that he
calleth it the kingdom of heaven. For be there never so
much cockle in that field, yet doth God continually out
of that field with his fan, cleanse from the cockle good
corn and sendeth it pure and clean into heaven and in
that field like as the devil turneth the corn into cockle,
so God turneth again much cockle into corn. And this
marvellous strange turning never ceaseth nor never shall
while the world endureth. *(826)*

9. We may not look at our pleasure to go to heaven
in feather beds; it is not the way, for our Lord himself
went thither with great pain and by many tribulations,
which was the path wherein he walked thither, for the
servant may not look to be in better case than his master.
(14*)

10. And when we be discharged once of this gross
corruptible body that aggrieveth and beareth down the
soul and oppresseth the mind that many things thinketh
upon, then shall such folk as shall be saved, behold and
see the glorious godhead, the very clear solutions of
much inexplicable problems. *(1283)*

11. If we begin once to repent, we may be sure that
God offereth grace and will perfect our penance with
increase of his grace and will pardon the death due for our
deadly sin, but if we fail on our part to go forward with
his grace, and that we foolishly fall therefrom. *(545)*

12. In a council of Christian men the Spirit of God

inclineth every good man to declare his mind, and inclineth the congregation to consent and agree upon that that shall be best, either precisely the best, or the best at leastwise for the season; which whensoever it shall be better at any other time to change, the same spirit of God inclineth his Church either at a new council or by as full and whole consent as any council can have, to abrogate the first and turn it into the better. But when the council and the congregation agreeth and consenteth upon a point, if a few wilful folk, far the least both in number, wit, learning and honest living, would protest and say that themself would not agree, yet were their frowardness no hindrance with the determination or to the making of the law, but that it must stand still it be by another like authority changed. *(779)*

13. We say also that God rejoiceth and delighteth in justice and for that cause he delighteth to see a man so delight in the same and to take his sin so sorrowfully that he is content of himself by fasting and other affliction willingly to put himself to pain therefor. And I say that if God had not this delight, which is not a tyrannous but a good and godly delight, else would he put unto man no pain for sin at all. For it is plain false that God doth it for necessity of driving the sin out of the flesh because that otherwise it cannot be cured. For it is questionless that God can otherwise drive the sin out of the flesh and by other means cure it, if it so pleased him, and so would he, saving for his godly delight in justice, which he loveth to see man follow by fasting and other penance. *(372)*

14. Good men in their own mind conceive of the strength and fastness of the Catholic faith which they verily think so strong that heretics for all their babbling

shall never be able to vanquish. And therein undoubtedly their mind is not only good but also very true. But they think not far enough. For as the sea shall never surround and overwhelm all the land, and yet hath it eaten many places in and swallowed whole countries up, and made many places now sea that sometime were well inhabited lands and hath lost part of his own possession in other parts again: so though the faith of Christ shall never be overflown with heresies, nor the gates of hell prevail against Christ's Church, yet as in some places it winneth in new people, so may there in some places by negligence be lost the old. *(920)*

15. Nor am I sure though ye see some white sapphire or beryl so well counterfeit, and so set in a ring, that a right good jeweller will take it for a diamond, yet will ye not doubt for all that, but that there be in many other rings already set right diamonds indeed. Nor will ye not mistrust Saint Peter for Judas. Nor though the Jews were many so naughty that they put Christ to death, yet ye be wiser I know well than the gentlewoman was which in talking once with my father, when she heard that Our Lady was a Jew, first could not believe it, but said, "What ye mock, I think; I pray tell me the truth." And when it was so fully affirmed that she at last believed it, "And was she a Jew," quoth she, "so help me God, I shall love her the worse while I live." I am sure ye will not so, nor mistrust all for some, neither men nor miracles. *(137)*

16. When Jupiter, whom the poets fable for the great God, invited all the poor worms of the earth unto a great solemn feast that it pleased him upon a time to prepare for them, the snail kept her at home and would not come thereat. And when Jupiter asked her after

wherefore she came not at his feast, where he said she would have been welcome and have fared well and should have seen a goodly palace and been delighted with many goodly pleasures, she answered him that she loved no place as well as her own house. With which answer Jupiter grew so angry that he said since she loved her house so well, she should never after go from home, but should alway after bear her house upon her back wheresoever she went. And so hath she done ever since, as they say, and at the least wise I wot well she doth so now and hath done as long time as I can remember. Æsop meant by that feigned fable to touch the folly of such folk as so set their fantasy upon some small simple pleasure that they cannot find in their heart to forbear it, neither for the pleasure of a better man nor for the gaining of a better thing. By which their fond froward fashion they sometime fall in great indignation and take thereby no little harm. And surely such Christian folk as by their foolish affection which they have set like the snail upon there own house here, this earth, cannot for the loathness of leaving that house, find in their heart with their good will to go to the great feast that God prepareth in heaven, and of his goodness so gently calleth them to, be like, I fear, but if they mend that mind in time, to be served as the snail was yet much worse too. For they be like to have their house here, the earth, bound fast upon their backs for ever and not walk therewith where they will, as the snail creepeth about with hers, but lie fast bound in the midst with the foul fire of hell about them. For into this folly they bring themself by their own fault, as the drunken man bringeth himself into drunkenness, whereby the evil that he doth in his drunkenness is not forgiven him for his folly but to his pain imputed to his fault. *(1250)*

17. And albeit Christ forbode Saint Peter, being a priest, and under himself prince of his priests, to fight with the temporal sword toward the impeachment and resistance of his fruitful passion, whereupon depended the salvation of mankind, which passion our Saviour had before that time so sore reproved and rebuked in him that he called him therefore Satan, yet is it nothing to the purpose to allege that by that example temporal princes should without the hindrance of such spiritual profit and the sufferance of much spiritual harm, suffer their people to be invaded and oppressed by infidels, to their utter undoing not only temporal but also of a great perpetual, which were like of their frailty for fear of worldly grief and incommodity, to fall from the faith and deny their baptism. In which peril, since our Lord would not that any man should wilfully put himself and for that cause advised his disciples (Matt. 10, 23) that if they were pursued in one city they should not come forth and foolhardily put themselves in peril of denying Christ by impatience of some intolerable torments, but rather flee thence into some other place where they might serve him in quiet, till he should suffer them to fall in such point that there were no way of escape, and then would he have them abide by their weapons like mighty champions wherein they shall not in such case fail of his help. Now albeit so that Christ and his holy apostles exhort every man to patience and sufferance without requiting of an evil deed, or making any defence, but using further sufferance and doing also good for evil, yet neither doth this counsel bind a man that he shall of necessity against the common nature suffer another man causeless to kill him, nor letteth not any man from the defence of another whom he seeth innocent and invaded and oppressed by malice. In which case both nature, reason, and God's behest,

bindeth, first the prince to the safeguard of his people with the peril of himself as he taught Moses to know himself bounden to kill the Egyptians in the defence of the Hebrew, and after he bindeth every man to the help and defence of his good and harmless neighbour against the malice and cruelty of the wrongdoer. For as the holy Scripture saith, "God hath given every man charge of his neighbour to keep him from harm of body and soul as much as may lie in his power." And by this reason is not only excusable but also commendable that common war which every people taketh in the defence of their country against enemies that would invade it, since that every man fighteth not for the defence of himself, of a private affection to himself, but of a Christian charity for the safeguard and preservation of all other. *(278)*

18. Let us then evermore make ourself ready for death nothing left undone that where Our Saviour said after all his sermons ended that after two days he should be delivered to be crucified, we may by help of his grace say to ourself and our friends every day, "I have done all my business that I am come in to this world for." *(1299)*

19. Truth it is that no man can with all the reason he hath in such wise change the nature of pain that in the having of pain he feel it not. For, but if it be felt, it is, indeed, no pain. And that is the natural cause for which a man may have his leg stricken off by the knee and grieve him not if his head be off but half an hour before. But reason may make a reasonable man (though he would not be so foolish as causeless to fall therein) yet upon good causes, either of gaining some kind of great profit, or avoiding some kind of great loss, or eschewing

thereby the suffering of far greater pain, not to shrink therefrom, and refuse it to his more hurt and harm, but for his far greater advantage and commodity, content and glad to sustain it. And this doth reason alone in many cases, where it hath much less help to take hold of than it hath in this matter of faith. For well you wot, to take a sour and bitter potion is a great grief and displeasure and to be lanced and have the flesh cut is no little pain. Now when such things shall be ministered unto a child or to some childish man either, they will by their own wills rather let their sickness or their sore grow unto their more grief till it become incurable than abide the pain of the curing time, and that for faint heart joined with lack of discretion. But a man that hath more wisdom, though he would without cause no more abide the pain willingly than would the other yet since reason sheweth him what good he shall have by the suffering and what harm by the refusing, this maketh him well content, and glad also for to take it. *(1253)*

20. Now knoweth every man very well that all the pith of a man's living standeth not in only teaching. For many be full well taught how they should live, yea, and so well taught, that they be able to teach it other full well and live themself full nought. We shall not need to seek long for example since no man doubteth that Judas Iscariot had so good a schoolmaster and was with him so long that if he had any wit he was fitly well taught how he should live. And that he was not all witless, though lacking of good will, he grew in conclusion graceless, appeareth well in that so wise a master as Our Saviour was, sent him forth among other for one of his ushers to teach in his own time. And yet as well taught as he was, and as well as he taught other too, yet was his own living not very good while he was both a thief and a traitor to

God and man. And yet that we shall not need to seek so far as fifteen hundred year ago, I think it will be no great difficulty to find folk enough even now in our own time, that can preach and give good counsel to their neighbours against the vices in which they live themself. So that though to good living, good teaching be necessary, yet may every fool see that in good teaching standeth not all the pith of good living. *(585)*

21. He that in a sudden start of fear, or other feeling unadvisedly falleth and after, in labouring to rise again, comforteth himself with hope of God's gracious forgiveness, walketh in the ready way toward his salvation. But he that, with the hope of God's mercy to follow, doth encourage himself to sin and therewith offendeth God first—I have no power to shut the hand of God from giving out his pardon he list, nor would, if I could, but rather help to pray therefor—but yet I very sore fear that such a man may miss the grace to require it in such effectual wise as to have it granted. Nor I cannot suddenly now remember any example or promise expressed in Holy Scripture that the offender in such kind shall have the grace offered after in such wise to seek for pardon that God hath, by his other promises of remission promised to penitents, bound himself to grant it. *(1255)*

22. They tell of one that was wont alway to say that all the while he lived he would do what he pleased, for three words, when he died, should make all safe enough. But then so happened it that long ere he were old, his horse once stumbled upon a broken bridge, and as he laboured to recover him, when he saw it would not be but down into the flood headlong needs he should, in a sudden fright he cried out in the falling, "Have all to

the devil!" And there was he drowned with his three words ere he died whereon his hope hung all his wretched life. And therefore, let no man sin in hope of grace, for grace cometh but at God's will and that mind may be the hindrance that grace of fruitful repenting shall never after be offered him, but that he shall either graceless go linger on careless, or with a care fruitless, fall into despair. *(1174)*

23. Mark this well, for of this thing we be very sure that old and young, man and woman, rich and poor, prince and page, all the while we live in this world we be but prisoners and be within a sure prison out of which there can no man escape. And in worse case be we than those that be taken and imprisoned for theft. For they, albeit their heart heavily waiteth after the sessions, yet have they some hope either to break prison the while, or to escape there by favour, or after condemnation some hope of pardon. But we stand all in other plight; we be very sure that we be already condemned to death, some one, some other, none of us can tell what death we be doomed to, but surely can we all tell that die we shall. And clearly know we that of this death we get no manner pardon. For the King by whose high sentence we be condemned to die, would not of his death pardon his own Son. *(84)*

24. As for the railing fashion—if I durst tell so sad a man a merry tale, I would tell him of the friar that, as he was preaching in the country, spied a poor wife of the parish whispering with her pewfellow, and he, falling angry thereto, cried out unto her aloud, "Hold thy babble, I bid thee, thou wife in the red hood!" Which when the housewise heard, she became as angry again, that all the church rang thereon, "Marry, sir, I beshrew

his heart that babbleth most of us both. For I do but whisper a word with my neighbour, and thou hast babbled there all this hour!" *(948)*

25. If every man that can find a new found fantasy upon a text of Holy Scripture may have his own mind taken and his own exposition believed against the expositions of the old holy cunning doctors and saints, then may we surely see that none article of the Christian faith can stand and endure long. *(836)*

26. The words that Saint Paul rehearseth of the prophet Isaias prophesying of Christ's incarnation may properly be verified by the joys of heaven. For surely for the state of this world, the joys of heaven are by man's mouth unspeakable, to man's ears not audible, to man's heart unconceivable, so farforth excel they all that ever men have heard of, all that ever men can speak of, and all that ever any man can by natural possibility think on. And yet where the joys of heaven be such prepared for every saved soul, our Lord saith yet by the mouth of St John that he will give his holy martyrs that suffer for his sake many a special kind of joy. For he saith, "To him that overcometh I shall give him to eat of the tree of life" (Rev. 2. 7). *(1259)*

27. I beseech our Lord make us all so wise that we may every man here so wisely rule our self in this time of tears, this vale of misery, this simple, wretched world (in which as Boethius saith, one man to be proud that he beareth rule over other men, is much like as one mouse would be proud to bear a rule over other mice in a barn) God, I say, give us the grace so wisely to rule our self here, that when we shall hence in haste to meet the great Spouse, we be not taken sleepers and for lack

of light in our lamps, shut out of heaven among the very
foolish virgins. *(1434)*

28. If he were but a wayfaring man that I received into
my house as a guest, if he fall sick therein, and his
money gone, I reckon myself bounden to keep him
still, and rather to beg about for his relief than cast him
out in that case to the peril of his life what loss soever I
should happen to sustain in the keeping of him. For
when God hath by such chance sent him to me, and
there once matched me with him, I reckon myself
surely charged with him, till I may without peril of his
life be well and conveniently discharged of him. *(1209)*

29. I see well that you reckon that whoso dieth a
natural death, dieth like a wanton at his ease. You make
me remember a man that was once in a ship with us on
the sea, which while the sea was sore wrought and the
waves rose very high, and he came never on the sea
afore, and lay tossed hither and thither, the poor soul
groaned sore, and for pain he thought he would very
fain be dead and ever he wished, "Would God I were on
land that I might die in rest!" The waves so troubled
him there, with tossing him up and down, to and fro,
that he thought that trouble hindered him to die, because the waves would not let him rest, but if he might
once get to land, he thought he should then die there
even at his ease. By my troth, methinketh that the
death which men call commonly natural, is a violent
death to every man whom it fetcheth hence by force
against his will, and that is every man which, when he
dieth, is loath to die and fain would live longer if he
might. *(1256)*

30. What ease also call you this that we be bound to

abide all sorrow and shameful death and all martyrdom upon pain of perpetual damnation for the profession of our faith. Believe ye that these easy words of his easy yoke and light burden were not as well spoken to his apostles as to you, and yet what ease called he them to! Called he not them at watching, fasting, praying, preaching, walking, hunger, thirst, cold and heat, beating, scourging, emprisonment, painful and shameful death. The ease of his yoke standeth not in bodily ease, nor the lightness of his burden standeth not in the slackness of any bodily pain—except we be so wanton, that where himself had not heaven without pain, we look to come thither with play—but it standeth in the sweetness of hope, whereby we feel in our pain a pleasant taste of heaven. *(143)*

DECEMBER

1. *Our most dear Saviour Christ, which after the finishing of the old paschal sacrifice hast instituted the new sacrament of thine own blessed body and blood for a memorial of thy bitter passion, give us such true faith therein, and such fervent devotion thereto, that our souls may take fruitful spiritual food thereby. (1330)*

2. Our head is Christ and therefore to him must we be joined, and as members of his must we follow him if we will come thither. He is our guide to guide us thither and is entered in before us. And he therefore that will enter in after, "The same way that Christ walked, the same way must he walk" (1 John 2, 6). And what was the way by which he walked into heaven, himself sheweth what way it was that his Father had provided for him, where he said unto the two disciples going toward the castle of Emmaus, "Knew ye not that Christ must suffer passion and by that way enter into his kingdom?" (Luke 24, 26). Who can for very shame desire to enter into the kingdom of Christ with ease when himself entered not into his own without pain? *(1260)*

3. And surely albeit that some good man here and there, one among ten thousand, as Saint Paul and Saint Antony, and a few such other like, do live all heavenly, far out of all fleshly company as far from all occasion of worldly wretchedness, as from the common temple or parish church, yet, if churches and congregations of Christian people resorting together to God's service were once abolished and put away, we were like to have few good temples of God in men's souls, but all

would within a while wear away clean and clearly fall to nought. And this prove we by experience that those which be the best temples of God in their souls, they most use to come to the temple of stone. And those that least come there be well known for very ribalds and unthrifts, and openly perceived for temples of the devil. And this is not in our days only, but so hath been from Christ's days hither. I believe no man doubteth that Christ's apostles were holy temples of God in their souls and well understood the words of their master spoken to the woman of Samaria as the thing which their master after told them himself, or else how could some of them have written that communication which none of them heard as appeareth by the Gospel? But they not in their master's days only, but also after his resurrection and after that they had received the Holy Ghost and were by him instructed of every truth belonging to the necessity of their salvation, were not content only to pray secretly by themself in their chambers but also resorted to the temple to make their prayers. And in that place, as a place pleasant to God, did they pray in spirit and in truth, as well appeareth in the book of Saint Luke written of the acts of Christ's holy apostles. So that no doubt is there but that yet unto this day, and so forth to the world's end, it is and shall be pleasant unto God that this chosen people pray to him and call upon him in temple and church. Whereof himself witnesseth with the prophet, "My house shall be called a house of prayer" (Matt. 21, 13). *(122)*

4. Nor God remitteth not the sins of his chosen people, nor forbeareth not to impute the blame thereof unto them because they be his chosen people. For he accepteth not folk for their persons but for their merits, but whereas they have sinned, he punisheth as well them

as other, and sometime more, because their former good
living somewhat of congruence deserved that they
should by punishment be called again to grace, and not
be for their fault so soon cast clean away as some other,
obdurate in malice and evil custom of sin, deserve to
have the grace of God and his calling on never more
offered unto them, and unto some it is offered that will
not receive it. God called on David by the prophet
Nathan and yet punished his offence. Christ looked on
Peter after he had forsaken and forsworn him, and Peter
therewith took repentance. God looked on Judas and
kissed him too and he turned to none amendment. Now
God from the beginning before the world was created,
foreseeing in his divine prescience, or rather in the
eternity of his Godhead, presently beholding that Peter
would repent and Judas would despair and that the one
would take hold of his grace and the other would reject
it, accepted and chose the one and not the other, as he
would have made the contrary choice if he had foreseen
in them the contrary chance. *(272)*

5. Whensoever we grow perverse and choose no longer
to follow the spirit, but fall into the flesh and walk in
the works thereof and thereby put the spirit out of his
dwelling, then cease we to be the sons of God were we
never so dear darlings to him before, and shall never
be his sons again until we mend again and leave this
flesh again and fall again to the spirit. *(700)*

6. Eye-flattering fortune, look thou never so fair,
   Nor never so pleasantly begin to smile,
   As though thou wouldst my ruin all repair,
   During my life thou shalt not me beguile.
   Trust I shall God, to enter in a while
   His haven of heaven, sure and uniform;
   Ever after thy calm look I for a storm. *(40*)*

7. Special verses may there be drawn out of the Psalter against the devil's wicked temptations, as for example, "Let God arise, and let his enemies be scattered: let them also that hate him flee before him" (Ps. 67). And many other, which are in such horrible temptation to God most pleasant and to the devil very terrible, but none more terrible nor more odious to the devil than the words with which our Saviour drove him away himself— "Begone, Satan!" (Matt. 4, 10)—nor no prayer more acceptable unto God nor more effectual for the matter than those words which our Saviour hath taught us himself: "And lead us not into temptation, but deliver us from evil." *(1198)*

8. God sent men hither to wake and work and as for sleep and gaming (if any gaming be good in this vale of misery in this time of tears) it must serve but for a refreshing of the weary body, to renew it unto watch and labour again, not all men in bodily labour, but as the circumstances of the persons be, so to be busied in one good business or other. *(1048)*

9. Let them a' God's name speak as lewdly as they list of me, and shoot never so many arrows at me as long as they do not hit me, what am I the worse? But if they should once hit me, I have more cause, I assure thee, to pity them than to be angry with them. *(13*)*

10. God in the creation of man gave to him two states; one, competent and convenient for his mortal nature, another of special grace a farther state of special prerogative, that is to wit, the possibility of immortality put in his own hand, and of the obtaining of eternal bliss in heaven, of which two things there was neither naturally pertaining to him. *(1284)*

11. When we hear the Scripture or read it, if we be not rebellious but endeavour ourself to belief and captive and subdue our understanding to serve and follow the faith, praying for God's gracious aid and help, God then worketh with us and inwardly doth incline our heart unto the assent of the thing that we read, and after a little spark of our faith once had, encreaseth the credence in our incredulity. *(579)*

12. But in matters of belief and faith, which be truths revealed and declared by God unto man, though that in diverse times there may be more things farther and farther revealed, and other than were disclosed at the first, yet can there never anything be by God revealed after that can be contrary to anything revealed by himself before. *(779)*

13. But since the goodness of God provideth that his grace is ever ready to him that will use it, therefore, though the will of man may nothing do without grace, yet without any speaking of grace, we commonly let not to say, man may do this, and man may do that, as believe, and hope, and love, and live chaste, and do alms and fast, and many such other things, not meaning, though we make no mention of grace, that man can therefore do them without grace. Like as we say that a man may see to thread a needle and speak nothing of the light, and yet mean we not that he can thread it in the dark. *(582)*

14. For pride is, as Saint Austin saith, the very mother of heresies. For of an high mind to be in the liking of the people, hath come into many men so mad a mind and so frantic that they have not cared what pain they took without any other recompense or reward,

but only the fond pleasure and delight that themself conceive in their heart when they think what worship that people talketh of them. And they be the devil's martyrs, taking much pain for his pleasure, and his very apes, whom he maketh to tumble through the hope of the holiness that putteth them to pain without fruit. And yet often times maketh them miss of the vain promise whereof only they be so proud. For while they delight to think they be taken for holy, they be many times well perceived and taken for hypocrites, as they be. But such is this cursed affection of pride and so deep setteth in the claws where it catcheth, that hard it is to pull them out. This pride hath ere this made some learned men to devise new fantasies in our faith because they would be singular among the people. *(282)*

15. But since that upon Saint Peter's first confession of the right faith that Christ was God's son, our Lord made him his universal vicar and under him head of his Church, and that for his successor he should be the first upon whom and whose firm confessed faith he would build his Church and of any that was only man make him the first and chief head and ruler thereof, therefore he showed him that his faith, that is to say the faith by him confessed, should never fail in his Church, nor never did it, notwithstanding his denying. For yet stood still the light of faith in Our Lady, of whom we read in the Gospel continual assistance to her sweetest son without fleeing or flitting. And in all other we find either fleeing from him one time or another, or else doubt of his resurrection after his death, his dear mother only except, for the signification and remembrance whereof the Church yearly in the Tenebræ lessons leaveth her candle burning still when all the remnant, that signifieth his apostles and disciples, be one by one

put out. And since his faith in effect failed, and yet the faith that he professed abode still in Our Lady, the promise that God made was, as it seemeth, meant to him but as head of the Church. And therefore Our Lord added thereto, "And thou being one of these days converted, confirm and strengthen thy brethren." In which by these words Our Saviour meant and promised that the faith should stand for ever. So that the gates of hell should not prevail there against. *(143)*

16. How many Romans, how many noble courages of other sundry countries have willingly given their own lives and suffered great deadly pains and very painful deaths for their countries and the respect of winning by their deaths the only reward of worldly renown and fame? And should we then shrink to suffer so much for eternal honour in heaven and everlasting glory? *(1261)*

17. Let us conform our will unto his, not desiring to be brought unto the peril of persecution (for it seemeth a proud high mind to desire martyrdom) but desiring help and strength of God if he suffer us to come to the stress either being sought, found, or brought out against our wills, or else being by his commandment, for the comfort of our cure, bounden to abide. *(1262)*

18. So is it also true that all the faith we have, or can have, can of his own nature as little or much less deserve heaven as our other good deeds. For what great thing do we do to God or what great thing could we ask of him of right, because we believe him, as though his worship hung in our hands and his estimation lost if he were out of credence with us? *(270)*

19. Let us fall to fasting, to prayer, to almsdeed in

time and give that unto God that may be taken from us. If the devil put in our mind the saving of our land and our goods, let us remember that we cannot save them long. If he fear us with exile and fleeing from our country, let us remember that we be born into the broad world, and not like a tree to stick in one place, and that whithersoever we go, God shall go with us. *(1262)*

20. It is but a feigned faith for a man to say to God secretly that he believeth him, trusteth him, and loveth him, and then openly, where he should to God's honour tell the same tale, and thereby prove that he doth so, there to God's dishonour, as much as in him is, flatter God's enemies, and do them pleasure and worldly worship, with the forsaking of God's faith before the world, and is either faithless in his heart too, or else knoweth well that he doth God this despite even before his own face. For except he lack faith, he cannot but know that Our Lord is everywhere present, and, while he so shamefully forsaketh him, full angrily looketh on. *(1255)*

21. When we feel us too bold, remember our own feebleness. When we feel us too faint, remember Christ's strength. In our fear let us remember Christ's painful agony that himself would for our comfort suffer before his passion, to the intent that no fear should make us despair. And ever call for his help, such as himself list to send us, and then need we never to doubt but that either he shall keep us from a painful death, or shall not fail so to strength us in it that he shall joyously bring us to heaven by it. And then doth he much more for us than if he kept us from it. For as God did more for poor Lazarus in helping him patiently to die for hunger at the rich man's door than if he had brought

him to the door all the glutton's rich dinner, so though he be gracious to a man whom he delivereth out of painful trouble, yet doth he much more for a man if through right painful death he deliver him from this wretched world into eternal bliss. *(1263)*

22. For God is not bounden to the place, nor our confidence bounden to the place, but unto God, though we reckon our prayer more pleasant to God in the Church than without because his high goodness accepteth it so; in likewise do not we reckon Our Lord bounden to the place or image where the pilgrimage is, though we worship God there because himself liked so to have it. *(123)*

23. Ye be proud of the arms of your ancestors set up in the prison, and all your pride is because ye forget that it is a prison. For if ye took the matter aright, the place a prison, yourself a prisoner condemned to death from which ye cannot escape, ye would reckon this gear as worshipful as if a gentleman thief when he should go to Tyburn would leave for a memorial the arms of his ancestors painted on a post in Newgate. Surely, I suppose that if we took not true figure for a fantasy but reckoned it as it is indeed, the very express fashion and manner of all our estate, men would bear themselves not much higher in their hearts for any rule or authority that they bear in this world, which they may well perceive to be indeed no better but one prisoner bearing a rule among the remnant as the tapster doth in the Marshalsea, or at the uttermost, one so put in trust with the gaoler that he is half an under-gaoler over his fellows till the sheriff and the cart come for him. *(84)*

24. For rest and recreation should be but as a sauce.

And sauce should, ye know well, serve for a faint and weak stomach to get it the more appetite to the meat and not for increase of voluptuous pleasure in every greedy glutton that hath in himself sauce malapert already enough. And therefore likewise as it were a fond feast that had all that table full of sauce and so little meat therewith that the guests should go thence as empty as they came thither, so it is surely a very mad ordered life that hath but little time bestowed in any fruitful business and all the substance idly spent in play. *(1048)*

25. And therefore, can we not doubt if we follow God and with faithful hope come run unto him, but that he shall in all matter of temptation take us near unto him, and set us even under his wing, and then are we safe if we will tarry there. For against our will can there no power pull us thence nor hurt our souls there. *(1179)*

26. The Church worshippeth not saints as God but as God's good servants, and, therefore, the honour that is done to them redoundeth principally to the honour of their master, like as in common custom of people we do reverence sometime and make great cheer to some men for their master's sake whom else we would not perhaps bid once good morrow. *(118)*

27. In bearing the loss of worldly goods, in suffering of captivity, thraldom and imprisonment, and in the glad sustaining of worldly shame, if we would in all those points deeply ponder the example of Our Saviour himself, it were of itself alone sufficient to encourage every kind of Christian man and woman to refuse none of all those calamities for his sake. *(1260)*

28. To all good Christian people. In most piteous wise

continually calleth and crieth upon your devout charity and most tender pity for help and comfort, and relief your late acquaintance, kindred, spouses, companions, play-fellows and friends and now your humble and un-acquainted and half-forgotten suppliants, poor prisoners of God, silly souls in Purgatory here abiding and enduring the grievous pains and hot cleansing fire that corrodes and burneth out the rusty and filthy spots of sin, till the mercy of Almighty God, the rather by your good and charitable means, vouchsafe to deliver us hence. *(288)*

29. Either first the Church hath the truth and belief all one way until some or some few begin the change, and then though all be yet of the Church, till some by their obstinacy be gone out or put out, yet is it no doubt but if I will believe the Church, I must still believe them that still believe that way that all the whole believed before. Or else, if there were any thing that was per-adventure such that in the Church sometime was doubted and reputed for unrevealed and unknowen, if, after that, the holy Church fall in one consent upon the one side, either by common determination at a general council, or by a perfect persuasion and belief so received through Christendom that the Christian people think it a damnable error to believe the contrary, then, if any would after take a contrary way, were it one or more, were it few or many, were they learned or unlearned, were they lay people or of the clergy, yet can I nothing doubt which part to believe if I will believe the Church. *(167)*

30. Would God, as I many times have said, that the remembrance of Christ's kindness in suffering his passion for us, the consideration of hell that we should

fall in by forsaking of him, the joyful meditation of eternal life in heaven, that we shall win with this short temporal death patiently taken for him, had so deep a place in our breast, as reason would they should, and as (if we would do our duty toward it and labour for it and pray therefor) I verily think they should. For then should they so take up our mind and ravish it all another way, that as a man hurt in a fray feeleth not sometime his wound nor yet is ware thereof till his mind fall more thereon, so far forth, that sometime another man sheweth him that he hath lost an hand, before he perceive it himself, so the mind ravished in the thinking deeply of those other things, Christ's death, hell and heaven, were likely to diminish and put away of our painful death four parts of the feeling either of the fear, or the pain. *(1261)*

31. *Give me thy grace, good Lord,*
 To set the world at nought;
 To set my mind fast upon thee,
 And not to hang upon the blast of men's mouths;
 To be content to be solitary;
 Not to long for worldly company;
 Little and little utterly to cast off the world,
 And rid my mind of all the business thereof;
 Not to long to hear of any worldly things,
 But that the hearing of worldly fantasies may be to
 me displeasant;
 Gladly to be thinking of God;
 Piteously to call for his help;
 To lean unto the comfort of God;
 Busily to labour to love him;
 To know mine own vility and wretchedness;
 To humble and meeken myself under the mighty hand
 of God;

To bewail my sins passed;
For the purging of them, patiently to suffer adversity;
Gladly to bear my purgatory here;
To be joyful of tribulations;
To walk the narrow way that leadeth to life;
To bear the cross with Christ;
To have the last thing in remembrance;
To have ever afore mine eye my death that is ever at hand;
To make death no stranger to me;
To foresee and consider the everlasting fire of hell;
To pray for pardon before the judge come;
To have continually in mind the passion that Christ suffered for me;
For his benefits uncessantly to give him thanks;
To buy the time again that I before have lost;
To abstain from vain confabulations;
To eschew light foolish mirth and gladness;
Recreations not necessary to cut off;
Of worldly substance, friends, liberty, life and all, to set the loss at right nought, for the winning of Christ;
To think my most enemies my best friends;
For the brethren of Joseph could never have done him so much good with their love and favour as they did him with their malice and hatred.
These minds are more to be desired of every man, than all the treasure of all the princes and kings, Christian and heathen, were it gathered and laid together all upon one heap. (1416)

SUBJECT INDEX

*This book was originally published as
"The Heart of Thomas More"
by Burns Oates Ltd, London*